FAMILY
SURVIVAL
IN AN X-RATED WORLD

ADRIAN ROGERS
and STEVE ROGERS

FAMILY SURVIVAL
IN AN X-RATED WORLD

A PRACTICAL PROGRAM for GUARDING YOUR HEART and PROTECTING YOUR HOME

Foreword by **ZIG ZIGLAR**

This work is lovingly dedicated to my birth family—my
parents, A. D. and Rose Rogers, along with my sister, Alliean, and
my brothers, Arden and Barry.
Next, it is dedicated to Joyce, the wonderful girl I married,
and the five children she has given to me: Steve, Gail, Phillip
(now in heaven), David, and Janice. Along with these come sons
and daughters-in-law, and a tribe of the greatest grandkids in the
world. I love you all.

Adrian Rogers

To the three wonderful women in my life:
Mom, thanks for your prayers and encouragement.
My wife, Cindi, thanks for loving me for over thirty years.
My daughter, Renae, I bless you with love and joy throughout
your life. I love you all.

Steve Rogers

978–0–8054–2693–9

Published by B&H Publishing Group
Nashville, Tennessee

Dewey Decimal Classification: 306.7
Subject Heading: INTERNET PORNOGRAPHY \
COMPUTER SEX \ INTERNET—SECURITY MEASURES

Unless otherwise indicated Scripture text is quoted from the New King James Version, copy-
right © 1979, 1980, 1982, Thomas Nelson, Inc., Publishers. Other versions are identified as
follows: KJV, King James Version. Phillips, reprinted with permission of Macmillan Publishing Co., Inc. from J. B. Phillips: The New Testament in Modern English, revised edition, ©
J. B. Phillips 1958, 1960, 1972.

3 4 5 6 7 8 9 10   17 16 15 14 13

Contents

Foreword

There is a battle being waged for the hearts and minds of our children in this X-rated society. Parents desperately need practical help. This book is so valuable because it doesn't just tell us what and why, but it shows us how.

This marvelous new book, *Family Survival in an X-rated World*, offers hope, direction, and encouragement for all of us. It is indeed a powerful action plan for family survival in an x-rated world. Dr. Rogers identifies the problems we face in our society and then provides the solutions to achieve the victory that will enable us to have a richer family life, a more fulfilling personal life, and to make contributions to our community.

This is a message of legitimate hope—which is the foundational quality of all change—that provides encouragement and the fuel on which hope runs. We are taught how to guard our hearts, which control the issues of life. Very practical advice is given on how to have a clean thought life.

Dr. Rogers warns of the pornographic saturation on the Internet, as well as its presence in television, movies, videos, and DVDs that can destroy our lives and the lives of our loved ones. Then, he teaches us how to win this battle for our minds and hearts. This is more than psychology. It is biblical truth.

One more time I remind you that in this joy-filled book, Pastor Rogers points out not just good ways to do things, but the best ways to follow God's admonitions, obey his Word, and worship his Son.

The reader will find many inspiring phrases, ideas, quotes, examples, directions, and scriptural references in this book that you will want to make note of so that you can embrace and incorporate them in your daily life.

Ralph Waldo Emerson said, "What lies behind you and what lies before you are tiny matters compared to what lies within you." Here is a book that will reveal what lies inside of you and how to use it to lift yourself up to that higher ground where the view is more beautiful, encouraging, exciting, and peaceful. Your benefits, regardless of age or occupation, will be a more joyful life and the godly home that God wants you to have. This joy and a godly home will energize you like nothing else can or will.

Family Survival in an X-rated World is loaded with God's love and will enable you to glorify God and enable him to use you in your life to benefit others in your journey through this uncertain world in which we live.

One more personal word—when I was a new Christian, Dr. Adrian Rogers had a powerful impact on my walk with Christ. His personal example and biblical wisdom, which have earned my love, respect and gratitude, continue to impact my life as well as the lives of countless thousands of others.

God bless you as you read, devour, use, and follow the marvelous processes that Dr. Rogers presents.

Zig Ziglar
Author and Motivational Teacher

Preface

Some books tell "what" and "why." Others show you "how." This book is written not to tell you what, but to show you *how.* Our desire is to be extremely practical and helpful as you seek to guard your heart and protect your home from pornography.

To combat the threat of terrorism within its borders, the United States created the Department of Homeland Security on October 8, 2001. Its purpose is to protect the country's borders from evil fanatics who want to harm American citizens by any means possible. One of the greatest fears is that terrorist groups might explode a so-called "dirty bomb"—a conventional explosive packaged with radioactive materials such as plutonium—in a major urban area in the United States.

Indeed, the world we live in is a dangerous place. However, there is another enemy—more insidious than political terrorism—that you face as a parent. It is not a threat from a dirty bomb, but from dirty pictures, dirty Web sites, dirty movies, and dirty TV. The "terrorists" behind this threat owe no allegiance to a political or religious agenda. Their creed is greed; they are motivated solely by selfishness. Their goal is the complete destruction of the hearts and minds of your family.

To combat this X-rated environment in which we all live, you need to create your own "department of homeland security." Mom and Dad are the cabinet level positions that report directly to the Chief. Your job is to protect and defend at all costs the innocence of your children, to keep them safe from stalkers and predators, and to secure the borders of your home against outside invasion.

In this battle, you will need weapons and ammunition. That is why this book was written. It contains the weapons and ammunition you will need—knowledge, truth, conviction, boldness, and encouragement—to engage the enemy head-on. It is filled with specific instructions to create and deploy your own spiritual "smart bombs" on Satan's strongholds.

This volume is really a book meant to bring encouragement rather than guilt. It is not a depiction of the lurid and seamy aspects of pornography. Therefore, you can read and enjoy it together with your family. It can be used by men's and women's groups or youth groups in churches without fear of embarrassment.

We send this volume with prayer and expectancy that you will learn, be encouraged, and put into practice what you have learned. Our desire for you is that your personal life and that of your children will enjoy God's great plan for your family, and you will experience a healthy, happy, and holy lifestyle together.

Adrian Rogers
Steve Rogers

PART I

The Battle
We Face

War on the Home

Watch Out!

A Tsunami Is Heading Your Way

A tsunami of sludge has hit the shores of America, and it is at the very doorstep of your home. You may be alarmed if you knew what is now seeping under the threshold. You may just *think* that your family is all safe and secure inside. Imagine the following:

It's 10:30 P.M. Sam Richards walks into his daughter's bedroom to tell her to turn out the lights and get into bed. Natalie is a bright-minded, thirteen-year-old, who is the emotional heartbeat of her proud father. Natalie has her back to the door and does not hear her father enter the room that is semidark. The blue light of the ever-present computer is giving most of the light out into the room.

Sam glances at the screen and the blood drains from his face. There in vivid color and detail is the grossest kind of hardcore porn. Sam considers himself to be reasonably sophisticated, but he is flattened by what he sees. And there looking on is thirteen-year-old Natalie.

Emotions come like a torrent to Sam—shock, rage, fear, anger and bewilderment. "Natalie, what are you watching?" Natalie quickly tries to remove the images and turns to her father, "Dad, I was doing my homework on the computer and this stuff just came up. I was trying to get it off when you came in."

Sam wanted to believe Natalie. It was difficult for him to think that Natalie would have intentionally visited such a Web site. Sam muttered some words to Natalie. He really could not remember much of what he said because his mind was almost numb. His gut reaction was to bring an axe into the bedroom and smash the computer like it was a vicious animal tearing at his daughter's throat.

The next morning there was the conversation that one might expect—questions, promises, prayers, and warning. But the worst was yet to come.

Sam asked a friend at work who was computer savvy to come to his house and put a filter on Natalie's computer. The friend asked, "Would you like for me to do a search to find out what sites she has visited before?" Sam agreed, and his worst fears were then confirmed. Natalie was a regular visitor to these pornographic sites.

Consider another scenario. Joan goes into Eric's room to change the sheets on her fourteen-year-old son's bed. Her morning was uneventful until she pulled off a sheet and some magazines fell

*Today's kids
are becoming roadkill
on the information
superhighway.*

on the floor. They had been stashed under the mattress. Joan picked them up and turned a few pages. Her heart sank. How could a fourteen-year-old get hold of such filthy magazines?

When Eric came home from school, she had the magazines on the kitchen table. When he saw them, he looked stunned and stood with his head down. "Eric, where did you get these?" "Mom, they don't belong to me. I was keeping them for a friend." The talk, however, continued and came to a climax when Eric finally confessed that they were his. Perhaps, the worst thing followed when he said, "Mom, what's the big deal? All of the guys I know have magazines like this."

Finally, consider this. Meg was having a sleepover at her house. The five girls invited were all members of the same Sunday School class. They did what teens normally do. They laughed, sang, called some friends on the cell phone and at 10:30 put a DVD in to watch a movie. It was one that Beverly brought. It was a part of her family's collection of DVDs. Meg settled down on the floor to watch. The movie started out all right, but soon a seamy love scene laced with profanity and vulgarisms appeared. Meg blushed. She was shocked and surprised that Beverly would bring such a movie into her house—especially when all of the girls present were members of the same Sunday School class. Meg wanted to turn it off immediately, but she sat frozen. Should she embarrass Beverly? Was she herself too prudish to watch? And after all, the DVD belonged to Beverly's parents.

Awash in a Cesspool of Sludge

These stories are only illustrations of what is being played over and over in thousands of homes today. This subterranean river of slime has erupted, and the wave has hit. Material that was once sold in back alleys is now on open display in magazine racks and neighborhood drug stores. It is being piped into the homes of America's families through cable television. And beyond all of that, the most dangerous and insidious of all is the Internet, which has become part of daily life in almost every home and classroom.

This battle is so critical because Satan wants to pollute a child's mind, to corrupt that child, to steal from that child the very best—the future marital happiness that God wants for him. Our children today have to walk through a mud-slide of filth and depravity. It's heart-breaking.

My purpose in this book is not to convince you that pornography is out there. If you need convincing, somehow you are numb. You are not awake. It is there. In doing research for this book, I have not looked at pornography. I don't intend to, and I don't have to. I don't have to eat swill to write a book on hogs. But I have enough awareness of the problem to know what is going on.

Sewers in the Streets

Some people say, "Well, it's only natural. That's the way God made us." Paul Harvey responds this way: "I am opposed to putting garbage on television for the same reason I would oppose open sewers in our streets. It can be argued that what is in these sewers is natural and normal and everybody does it. And that it is not dirty. But everywhere in the world where sewage flows unconfined, it breeds disease."

And yet the American appetite for pornography seems almost insatiable. It seems like a sewer has broken open over America.

In 1973, Americans spent no more than ten million dollars on pornography in a year. By 2000, Americans were spending ten *billion* a year. That is a 1,000-percent increase in pornography. At this writing, the problem is still growing.

This is sad for adults, but it's even sadder for children. Today's kids are being systematically seduced. They're becoming roadkill on the information superhighway. The hardening and destructive force is beyond our power to estimate and to state.

Prime Time Has Become Slime Time

Two hours of so-called entertainment filled with illicit sex and profanity. No doubt we are talking about an R-rated Hollywood movie, right? Wrong! We're talking about the prime-time television hours.

According to a 2003 report by the Parents Television Council, foul language in the prime-time television hours has increased dramatically between 1998 and 2002:

- Foul language during ABC's family hour (8 to 9 P.M.) increased by 61.7 percent.
- Foul language during the family hour on CBS increased an astounding 471.3 percent.
- Foul language on NBC shot up across the board, in every study period and in every time slot—up 114.7 percent

during the family hour, 59.4 percent during the 9:00 P.M. ET/PT time slot, and 174 percent in the 10:00 P.M. ET/PT time slot.

In addition to profanity and foul language, sexual content has risen dramatically on television. Pediatrician and author Victor Strausberger put it this way: "The average American teenager views almost 15,000 sexual jokes, innuendos and other references on TV each year. Fewer than 170 of these deal with what any sane adult would define as responsible sexual behavior . . . Add to that the 20,000 commercials per year each teenager in America sees— with implicit messages that sex is fun and everyone out there is having sex but you—and you have at least the possibility of a fairly important influence."

L. Brent Bozell, president of the Parents Television Council, sums it up like this: "The debate is over and the verdict is in—by poisoning the Family Hour, the networks and their affiliates, with the generous support of sponsors, are robbing children of their innocence. Moreover, they do so without any sense of shame. It must stop."

A Sticky Web, a Deadly Trap

Satan has set a deadly trap for his unwary victims. Like a spider's web is the sticky trap of pornography. The spider first snares an insect. The next step is to wrap it securely with more sticky strands and finally to suck the life juice from its victim. This is so much like porn.

The letters TRAP remind us of the deadly effects of porn. Let's make an acrostic:

Temptation

Repetition

Addiction

Participation

Temptation. The exposure to porn often comes unexpectedly. A so-called friend shares his magazines. Graphic pictures appear on the computer screen. Unsolicited mail is delivered with soft- or hard-core porn. Both are seductive and dangerous. Porn can raise its ugly head almost anywhere. You don't have to go looking for it. It will find you. An innocent child may be pounced by this predator. Porn is in the air like a fungus.

Repetition. The curiosity factor and the hormonal drive begin to call for another look. Then there is the discovery of more and different enticement. There is certain sensual arousal and pleasure that seems to satisfy and yet call for more. Mental pictures make a groove in the mind.

Addiction. The addiction factor seems to come quickly for some. A very powerful desire for more and more deviant forms of pornography ensnares the participant. The willing victim begins to feed his or her imagination with this forbidden fruit. Yet the result is very much like drinking salt water to satisfy thirst. It is futile.

Participation. The user of porn will find ways to act out what has captured the mind. It may go no further than lustful fantasy, which Jesus called adultery in the heart. Or it may take the form of self-abuse or sexual aggression toward another. The user of porn will almost always find a way to participate in the twisted ideas that have saturated his mind and heart.

The bottom line is that he or she has been trapped in a very sticky web.

Satan's A-Team

Alvin Cooper, Ph.D., noted researcher on cybersex, has described the three "A"s of cybersex addiction: accessibility, anonymity, and affordability.[1] We call them "Satan's A-Team." They illustrate why pornography is so dangerous.

ACCESSIBILITY

Pornography today is so available. No longer are these things that you have to go out behind the barn to see—pictures that perhaps you would purchase in a plain wrapper from some unsavory person. The pornography is everywhere. You go to the corner market for a gallon of milk, and there's pornography. You stroll through the mall, and there is pornography. You go into a hotel, and there in the corner is a television set. Just change the channel— up comes the pornography.

The proliferation of pornography has become so widespread that *Penthouse* magazine recently filed for Chapter 11 bankruptcy. Long-time publisher Bob Guccione said even he is shocked by the bombardment of sexual material: "Today, there are triple-X videos, adult channels, and pay-per-view films; there are strip clubs, phone sex, and last of all, Internet sites that have no restrictions. Attractive women are flooding the porn market in a way that surprises even me."[2]

The easy availability of porn was eating away at his profits.

Alarmingly, studies have shown that boys ages 12 to 17 are the largest

∽

Porn can raise its ugly head almost anywhere. You don't have to go looking for it. It will find you.

∽

consumers of pornography in America, yet many parents refuse to believe that their children are involved in the use of pornography. But as an eight-to-ten-billion-dollars-a-year industry, the third largest revenue producer of organized crime in America, hard-core pornography boasts twenty thousand outlets around the country.[3]

AFFORDABILITY

Not since Manhattan Island was sold for twenty-four dollars by the Indians has so much dirt been sold so cheaply. It's affordable. Not only that, but mind-poisoning porn is free on many Internet sites. You don't even have to buy the dirt. It is dumped on you.

The pornographers are using the Internet as their current distribution system of choice. Everything that has ever been available in adult bookstores is now available for free, as teasers, without any minimum age. The pornographers have developed very sophisticated techniques, known as "page-jacking" and "mouse-trapping," to seduce users from wholesome sites into pornographic sites, and then to prevent their escaping from those pornographic sites.

ANONYMITY

And then you can watch it with anonymity—in a hotel room, in a bedroom with a computer. No longer do we ask, "It's 11:00 o'clock—do you know where your children are?" Now the question is "It's 4:30 in the afternoon. Do you know what your children are watching?"

Christians are not immune. The Maryland Coalition Against Pornography did a survey, and they found out that 40 to 60 percent of Christian men are involved in pornography in some way. Forty to 60 percent! Well, you say, those are just old codgers; what about the young people? Another survey of students at five Christian colleges found that 68 percent of male students said they had intentionally looked for pornography on the Internet. And we know that in these surveys about things like that, the respondents generally hedge the truth.

Safe Sex?

"Apologists for pornography hail voyeurism and self-gratification as the ultimate safe sex," says Gene Edward Veith in an article in *World* magazine entitled "The Pornographic Culture." No one is hurt, they say. No one can get AIDS from watching a video. Porn makes possible a kind of sexuality that is available for all, even the unattractive and socially inept. Porn allows sex to transcend the body, locating it instead in the mind. It frees sex from every moral constraint, without the limitations inherent in real-world entanglements. Porn makes it possible to have sex without any of the messy co.mplications of a relationship with another human being.

That is to say, pornography is the ultimate dehumanizing of sex. It is sex wholly and purposefully void of love. It takes what is designed for engendering new life and makes it sterile. It is Gnostic, like the old heresy—which combined permissiveness with contempt for the physical world—an assault against the body itself.[4]

Poison for the Mind and Heart

One of the deadliest poisons in the world actually comes from a frog. The toxin of the frogs comes out of pores in the skin. The

Phylobates terriblis lives in the rain forests of Central and South America. Its deadly poison is called Batrachotoxin, and one frog has enough in his body to kill twenty thousand mice or eight human beings. The poison frogs are also called poison-dart frogs because the Choco Indians from the Choco region in Colombia use them to poison their darts.

Satan has dipped his arrows into another kind of deadly poison and aimed them at the hearts of innocent kids. This poison does not cause immediate pain or death. To the contrary, it brings perverted pleasure and a slow death, but it is deadly.

We are at war! Satan is not playing games, nor should we. Thank God, there can be victory if we are willing to counterattack. Don't be intimidated by Satan's tsunamis or his poisoned arrows! Read on.

Endnotes

1. Alvin Cooper, Ph.D., "Cybersex—Getting Tangled in the Web," a presentation at the national council on Sexual Addiction and Compulsivity National Conference, April 1999 (quoted by Alan W. Aram in *Enrichment*, Winter 2001).

2. *Memphis Commercial Appeal*, August 20, 2003.

3. *Family Voice*, September 1993, p. 14.

4. Gene Edward Veith, *World*, April 7, 2001.

∾ 2 ∾

Heroes Wanted:
Apply Within

We all love heroes.

Whether they ride a white horse like the Lone Ranger, carry a bullwhip like Indiana Jones, or wield a light saber like Luke Skywalker, we are fascinated by them. Like Superman, our make-believe heroes are able to leap tall buildings in a single bound. Yet, real heroes, like the young shepherd David, are able to perform superhuman tasks, like facing a seemingly unconquerable opponent and defeating him with a simple slingshot and a stone from a brook.

Heroes, real or imagined, stand larger than life, never quit, and always persevere through apparently impossible odds. By the end of the book or movie, they will have managed to get the bad guy, save the world, and ride off into the sunset with the girl on the back of their horse!

Have you noticed that we have a hero shortage today? Not phony movie heroes. Real-life ones. Men and women who will stand head and shoulders above the crowd; parents who will face opposition and not back down; dads and moms who will look the enemy straight in the eye and not blink.

Heroes or Zeros?

In 1999, *Time* magazine conducted a poll to choose the "Person of the Century," the most influential human being of the last one hundred years. When the polls closed on January 19, 2000, Elvis Presley had gotten the most votes, eclipsing Billy Graham and Albert Einstein. Beatle John Lennon came in ahead of Mother Teresa, and Madonna ranked higher than Winston Churchill, Nelson Mandela, and Princess Diana.

In their quest for someone to admire, kids often mistake idols for heroes. Today's pop stars, movie idols, and superstar athletes fill the most admired list of teens, yet they openly warn, "Don't expect me to be a role model."

Today, it seems our kids take their cues on how to dress, how to talk, and how to think from those whose only real claim to "heroship" is chance genetics and a good agent. The entertainment world and the cultural elite prescribe what is cool and what is not, yet refuse to be held accountable to any standard of behavior or morality. Instead of being heroes, when it comes to having a life truly worth emulating, they are indeed zeros.

Do You Have What It Takes?

It is the challenge of parents to help their kids sort out the difference between idols and heroes; to help them realize that those who are admired simply because of how they look, what they sound like, or how high they can jump, are often the ones who make the biggest mess out of their lives.

It is also the challenge of parents to teach not only by word but by example. You can't lead your kids somewhere you have never been yourself. Determine to become someone they can look at and think, *I want to be just like you.*

A True Fish Tale

If there were a hero in the fish world, it would be the Pacific salmon. Guided by their innate navigation mechanisms, they leave the ocean and swim upstream, sometimes on a journey of hundreds of miles, to the spawning grounds where they were born. By the time they reach their destination, they will have scaled elevations of up to 2,200 feet. Along the way, they will jump waterfalls and relentlessly battle fierce downstream river torrents, all without food; spawning salmon don't eat once they begin their trip upstream. The ones who manage to elude the waiting predators and make the trip successfully are part of an elite group.

Today's pop stars, movie idols, and superstar athletes fill the most-admired list of teens, yet they openly warn, "Don't expect me to be a role model."

Only one in a thousand salmon hatchlings survive long enough to make it back to the spawning grounds. The ones that make it truly achieve hero status in the fish world.

Being a fish hero does not come without a price. Within a few weeks of spawning, the Pacific salmon will die—from sheer exhaustion. They literally give their lives for their offspring!

Dead Fish Floating

Any old dead fish can float downstream. It takes some backbone to swim against the current. Are you willing to go against the flow and fight for your family's survival? Jump a few waterfalls? Fight off a few grizzlies? Are you ready to "give your life" to the cause of protecting your home?

If you are, you will surely encounter resistance. Take a stand based on biblical principles, and you will find yourself swimming upstream alone. Being a hero doesn't mean that everyone will like you. In fact, what everyone else thinks really doesn't matter. That's because the heroes who are needed today don't need a costume and a cape. We don't need a superhero to save the world in one daring act of bravery.

What we *do* need are tens of thousands of parents who will be the heroes of their homes, dads and moms who will become champions for their children, who will stand with feet firmly planted and look the porn merchants square in the eye and resolutely proclaim: Not in our house!

It is our hope and prayer that by deciding to read this book, you have already accepted that challenge. In this chapter, we want to give you seven ways, from the book of Proverbs, that you can be a hero to your children.

Seven Steps to Becoming a Hero to Your Kids

1. A GODLY EXAMPLE

"The fear of the LORD is the beginning of knowledge, but fools despise wisdom and instruction. My son, hear the instruction of your father, and do not forsake the law of your mother; for they will be a graceful ornament on your head, and chains about your neck" (Prov. 1:7–9). "The righteous man walks in his integrity; his children are blessed after him" (Prov. 20:7).

Your children should learn from your example that you are the real deal. They will absorb far more from your lifestyle than from your lectures. You don't need to pretend perfection. If you do, you will come across as a phony. Your children do not want to know if you are perfect, but they do want to know that you are real. They want to know if you are genuine.

Therefore, you should let them see how you handle your mess-ups, failures, and problems. They will learn more from that than they will from phony perfectionism. Of course, the trouble with being a parent is that by the time you are experienced you usually are unemployed. Seriously, I want my children to see the same father in the home that they see in the pulpit.

Children pick up big and small things from the lifestyle of the parents. I was a grown man before I realized that I was constantly mispronouncing a word. I wondered why I did it, and then I heard my mother speak one day and it was the word that she mispronounced.

∽

Your children do not want to know if you are perfect, but they do want to know that you are real.

∽

Then I listened to my brothers and sister, and they mispronounced the same word.

Godly character needs to be demonstrated in the home. Integrity is the missing virtue among today's leaders. The emphasis today is on sports, grades, physical health, popularity, success, and ability, but not on character.

Ask yourself as a parent what qualities you would like to see God develop in your child? Think on these: contentment, courage, courtesy, discernment, fairness, friendliness, generosity, gentleness, helpfulness, honesty, humility, kindness, obedience, orderliness, patience, persistence, self-control, tactfulness, thankfulness, thriftiness, and wisdom.

Most every wise parent would say, "I want those character qualities in my children." So let us ask you this: Where will they learn these if they do not learn them in the home? We can't depend on the public schools, films, entertainment outlets, or even peers to teach these things. They are more caught than taught, and they are caught in the home.

2. UNCONDITIONAL LOVE

"Hear, my children, the instruction of a father, and give attention to know understanding; for I give you good doctrine: Do not forsake my law. When I was my father's son, tender and the only one in the sight of my mother, he also taught me, and said to me: 'Let your heart retain my words; keep my commands, and live'" (Prov. 4:1–4).

Fathers who have received love know how to give love. The problem today is that there are many who come from broken homes and have never known a father's love themselves. If you are a father like this, we have good news:. You can break that cycle.

Begin to show unconditional love to your children. Unconditional love is not giving them what they deserve but what they need. It really is a form of unconditional acceptance. This does not mean that you should accept the child's misbehavior, but you do accept the child. Your child should trust your love enough to share with you his or her failures.

In a very practical sense, this love needs to be demonstrated by physically touching them. This is what the father did to the prodigal when he came home: "And he arose, and came to his father. But when he was still a great way off, his father saw him and had compassion, and ran and fell on his neck and kissed him" (Luke 15:20).

A wise person has said, "Kids need hugs, not drugs." Keep your children from growing up thinking that hugs are only for sexual intimacy. Hug them affectionately, supportively, playfully, and tenderly. Let them see parents hugging one another in these ways. They may grow up believing that hugs are for sexual expression only, and in order to be hugged and huggable one must be physically attractive to the other hugger.

Charles Swindoll said it in a wonderful way:

> Many a young woman who opts for immoral sexual relationships does so because she can scarcely remember a time when her father so much as touched her.
> Unaffectionate dads, without wishing to do so, can trigger a daughter's promiscuity. All of this leads me to write

Unconditional love is not giving your children what they deserve but what they need. It really is a form of unconditional acceptance.

with a great deal of passion, "Dads, don't hold back your affection. Demonstrate your feelings of love and affection to both sons and daughters and don't stop once they reach adolescence. They long for your affirmation and appreciation. They will love you more for it. More importantly, they will emulate your example when God gives them their own family."

Another way to let your love be seen is in your sympathy for their hurts. Their hurts may seem small to you, but they may not be small to your child. Their pains are very real to them. Love tries to understand it and see it from the child's perspective. Even when it seems trivial, you might say, "I know it hurts. I hope it gets better."

In our family we have attended funerals for dogs and turtles and other animals. We have stood at the grave and wept with our children. We can tell you as parents we know what it is to hold a grown child in our arms and cry with them. There is a tremendous bonding.

3. Constant Encouragement

"My son, let them not depart from your eyes—keep sound wisdom and discretion; so they will be life to your soul and grace to your neck. Then you will walk safely in your way, and your foot will not stumble. When you lie down, you will not be afraid; yes, you will lie down and your sleep will be sweet. Do not be afraid of sudden terror, nor of trouble from the wicked when it comes; for the LORD will be your confidence, and will keep your foot from being caught" (Prov. 3:21–26).

You may bless your children in an incredible way with encouragement. When you regularly encourage, you give your kids confidence. We call this "blessing a child."

What do you ask the heavenly Father over and over again for? If you are like the average person, your prayer is, "Lord, bless me." Children want a blessing from their earthly father.

It has been said that kids need more strokes than pokes. Children need encouragement like a plant needs water. Try to catch them doing something right. Let them know, "I believe in you." Let your speech be primarily positive—constantly affirming.

Learn the difference between wise encouragement and pure praise. Encouragement is more powerful than praise. We are not sure where we got this idea, but it resonates with us. Be careful that the children don't get the conception that you love them because they got all As or even because they keep their room clean. They may get the idea that their personal worth depends on how they measure up. As a result, when performance goes down, self-image will go down with it. What is the difference between praise and encouragement? Praise may say, "You are great because you did something." Encouragement, however, says, "It's great that something was done, and I appreciate the way you did it."

Your child will say, "My mom and dad value me as a person. They appreciate my worth."

Never ever say to a child, "You'll never amount to anything." That may turn out to be a self-fulfilling prophecy. We have heard that Bill Glass, a prison evangelist, asks male prisoners, "How many of you had a father who said, 'One of these days you will end up in jail'?" Almost every one of them will lift their hand.

∽

Children need encouragement like a plant needs water. Try to catch them doing something right.

∽

4. WISE INSTRUCTION

"My son, if you receive my words, and treasure my commands within you, so that you incline your ear to wisdom, and apply your heart to understanding; yes, if you cry out for discernment, and lift up your voice for understanding, if you seek her as silver, and search for her as for hidden treasures; then you will understand the fear of the LORD, and find the knowledge of God. For the LORD gives wisdom; from His mouth come knowledge and understanding; He stores up sound wisdom for the upright; He is a shield to those who walk uprightly" (Prov. 2:1–7). "Train up a child in the way he should go, and when he is old, he will not depart from it" (Prov. 22:6).

Instruction must always be combined with training. To teach without training is to fail in your task. Notice that Scripture says, "Train up a child in the way he should go." It doesn't say, "Teach the child the way he should go." Instruction must always be combined with training. To teach without training is to fail in your task.

No one will ever learn to play the game of football by reading books about it.

> *To teach without training is to fail in your task. No one will ever learn to play the game of football by reading books about it.*

I was intrigued as I watched a man train a hunting dog. What patience and diligence he exhibited with that dog. Many people train a dog but then tie him up at night. They fail to train their kids and then turn them loose at night.

May we get a little personal here? How many parents who read this could give the Ten Commandments in order? Yet, if you are like many modern parents, you complain about the Ten Commandments not being posted in public places. We wonder—are we hypocrites? How many have the Ten Commandments posted in the home? Remember that the primary educational institution is the home.

Sadly, today's generation does not believe in a fixed standard of right and wrong. Fifty-eight percent of our young people cannot even say that there is an objective standard of truth. Eighty-five percent of our kids are liable to reason like this: "Just because it is wrong for you doesn't mean that it is wrong for me."

> ∾
>
> *Your child needs some goals and also some limitations. There are some things to be encouraged and some things to be denied.*
>
> ∾

Today's kids believe everything in life is negotiable. There is no firm distinction between right and wrong. The whole matter seems to be fluid.

5. REASONABLE RESTRICTION

"My son, keep your father's command, and do not forsake the law of your mother. Bind them continually upon your heart; tie them around your neck. when you roam, they will lead you; when you sleep, they will keep you; and When you awake, they will speak with you. For the commandment is a lamp, and the law is light; reproofs of instruction are the way of life" (Prov. 6:20–23).

Your child needs some goals and also some limitations. There are some things to be encouraged and some things to be denied. Remember that God gave limitations to Adam and Eve.

Strangely, it takes some restrictions to set children free. Limitations and restrictions will be tested by the child. He will push against them. If they move, he will have no security.

No limitation implies rejection to a child. If you don't conquer him, most likely, he will allow someone else to conquer him.

In this society restrictions are looked upon as something bad, but setting rules for families is one of the toughest and most crucial aspects of being a parent. Parents need to stop trying to win a popularity contest and learn to assume responsibility. Don't make too many rules, and keep the ones you make.

In our house there were two big rules. Number one: no dishonesty; number two: no disrespect. There were other rules but these were the big ones, and our kids knew it.

6. A LISTENING EAR

"He who answers a matter before he hears it, it is folly and shame to him. The spirit of a man will sustain him in sickness, but who can bear a broken spirit? The heart of the prudent acquires knowledge, and the ear of the wise seeks knowledge" (Prov. 18:13–15).

This is not always easy. You have to be ready to listen when they are ready to talk—not when it suits you to listen.

Sometimes when our oldest son would begin to talk and unburden his heart, Joyce and I would sit up until one o'clock or two o'clock in the morning because it was a golden moment and we didn't want to miss it.

Never be too busy to listen to a child, especially a hurting teenager. Build time to listen. One on one is great for listening. Take that child or grandchild alone for dinner or travel together.

While riding in the car, there may be miles of silence before the conversation begins.

You can't make it happen, so you must always be ready. Don't be in too big of a rush. We live in such a hurry with our computers, cell phones, call waiting, and instant messaging.

Learn to listen, and it will yield rich rewards.

7. A HAPPY ENVIRONMENT

"A merry heart makes a cheerful countenance, but by sorrow of the heart the spirit is broken. The heart of him who has understanding seeks knowledge, but the mouth of fools feeds on foolishness. All the days of the afflicted are evil, but he who is of a merry heart has a continual feast. Better is a little with the fear of the LORD, than great treasure with trouble. Better is a dinner of herbs where love is, than a fatted calf with hatred" (Prov. 15:13–17).

Keep your children happy, and be happy yourself. Mankind is God's only creation that laughs and weeps. The animals don't do this, but man is made in the image of God himself.

Verse 13 of Proverbs 15 teaches that "by sorrow of the heart the spirit is broken." The spirit that is spoken of is the true inner man. How sad it is when the inner person has been broken. The string has snapped, and the spark, zest, enthusiasm, and fight are gone.

Lighten up and brighten up. Remember what a wonderful gift wholesome laughter is. Notice also that verse 13 speaks of the countenance. We don't always have to laugh out loud to have a merry heart. Don't be ashamed of your sense of humor or your laughter. It has been documented that laughter along with a well-rounded sense of humor is one of the sure signs of intelligence.

Of course, laughter in the home should be clean and whole-some, not crude, cheap, or degrading. The Bible warns against this: "Neither filthiness, nor foolish talking, nor coarse jesting, which are not fitting, but rather giving of thanks" (Eph. 5:4). Obviously, children need to be taught when to laugh and when not to laugh. They ought to be able to say to their peers, "That's not funny. It's sick."

God filled Abraham's and Sarah's home with laughter: "And Sarah said, God hath made me to laugh, so that all that hear will laugh with me" (Gen. 21:6 KJV). Then God gave them a child, and they named that child Isaac, which means "laughter." In the book of Ecclesiastes we learn not only that there is a time to weep but a time to laugh. Your children need to see you laugh at yourself and also be able to laugh in times of trouble.

We had a ferocious hurricane in Florida. My father whom I admired so much was out helping the other men board up their windows. I was in the kitchen when he came in shivering, wet, cold, and exhausted. The power had gone off in our house, and my dad said to my mother, "I would give five dollars for a cup of coffee." My mother immediately began to fix coffee on the stove that was heated with gas. My father had forgotten that, and he had no idea that he could have a warm cup of coffee. When my mother served him that cup of coffee, he reached in his pocket, pulled out five dollars, and gave it to her. We all had a big laugh, and the storm did not seem nearly so threatening.

Laughter and humor can ease tension and manage fatigue. Husbands and wives who laugh together tend to stay together. Someone has called laughter "love with a funny bone." Learn to be firm, learn to be fair, and learn to be fun with your kids.

Are You Ready for the Challenge?

With these seven steps and the grace of God, your prospect of victory will be greatly enhanced. Remember, however, that these seven steps will not work unless you do.

Here is the question—are you ready for the challenge? Let us encourage you. It is a winnable fight, and the spoils of the battle are great. Indeed heroes are wanted. If you are ready to sign up for the battle, then read on.

～ 3 ～

Snakes in
the Playroom

I was riveted by a news article that told of a father's negligence that brought about the tragic death of his eight-year-old daughter. See if your heart aches like mine as you read the story.

GREENSBURG, Pa.—A man whose 8-year-old daughter was squeezed to death by the family's 11-foot python was found innocent Thursday of involuntary manslaughter but guilty of endangering the girl's welfare.

Robert Mountain, 31, was negligent but not grossly reckless in leaving Amber Mountain home alone with the snake last August, Judge Richard McCormick Jr. ruled in the nonjury trial. Mountain could get up to five years in prison.

Amber was found unconscious on the kitchen floor with the python, named Moe, coiled around her body. She died two days later in a hospital from compression of the head and neck.

The girl's mother—who bought the snake—pleaded guilty to child endangerment in December and was placed on probation for two years. Marcy Mountain testified against her husband; the two are estranged.[1]

Tragic indeed, but now let me share another "snake" tragedy. Not so spectacular, but also deadly in another realm. Consider the following.

The Nelsons are a family of four who have recently moved into an older three-bedroom house in a nice quiet neighborhood. The house seems to be in great shape except for the snake problem. Snakes have been getting in through a hole in the basement and have been turning up everywhere—in the bathrooms, the utility room, even the children's playroom.

Some of the snakes have been poisonous, so last week the mother went to the bookstore and bought a book on how to identify poisonous snakes. It even has color pictures showing the markings of coral snakes, rattlers, and cottonmouth moccasins.

Tonight, the mother and father are getting ready to go out to dinner with friends. Natalie has just turned fourteen and is ready to prove to her parents that she and little brother Christopher, eight, will be fine without a babysitter. Although Natalie is already babysitting for the McAllister twins across the street, mother still feels like a little last-minute admonition is in order.

"You have our cell phone if anything comes up. Make sure Christopher is in bed by nine, and Natalie, I'm leaving the snake book right here on the kitchen table. Do you promise me you won't play with any poisonous snakes while we're gone?"

"Yes, Mom, I promise," replies Natalie. "You know I'm a teenager. You don't have to treat me like a little kid."

"Better safe than sorry, dear. Keep an eye on Christopher."

"Not to worry, Mom. I won't let him anywhere near a snake."

Being the cautious parents that they are, the Nelsons call home from the restaurant to check on the kids. Christopher answers the phone. "Hi, Mom."

"Hi, Christopher. Everything OK?"

"No problem, Mom. I'm watching TV and Natalie is doing homework."

"You haven't been playing with any poisonous snakes, have you?"

"Well, this really cool looking one came in the den, and he let me pick him up, but I'm pretty sure he's not poisonous."

"Well, if there's any question at all, Christopher, look him up in the snake book. You know what I've told you . . ."

"I know, Mom. 'Better safe than sorry.' OK, I'll be in bed by nine. Love you too."

By now I hope you're thinking, *Do the Nelsons have rocks in their heads? Instead of buying a handbook on poisonous reptiles, why don't they spend the same fifteen dollars on a bag of concrete, a trowel, and a bucket, and patch the hole where the snakes are coming in?*

As ludicrous as the above scenario may sound, that is exactly how most parents today are dealing with the steady stream of poison that is coming right into the home on a daily basis. In fact, some parents are even paying someone to come out and install the snake hole for them!

The pay-per-view fare and the movie channels are the most dangerous. Television, if allowed, needs to be guarded and supervised. If it is not guarded, it should be discarded!

Also, I remind you that the television is not the only snake trail into the home, but it is a prevailing one. Later, we will discuss how to tame the TV. I warn you—it will take some courage.

Killers on the Loose

My wife, Joyce, and I got married after our first year in college. Soon after that, I was called to be the pastor of a little church. We drove 130 miles one way on weekends. Joyce was having some complications with a pregnancy, our first child. The doctor said it would not be good for her to travel that distance in the automobile.

It was Saturday and a news report came across the radio that there had been a prison break in a prison close to the trailer park where our little house trailer was sitting. People were told: "Lock your doors, lock your windows, take the keys out of your car, get the children off the streets, and be very, very careful. Of the three men who escaped, two were killers."

The prison was in the vicinity where we lived. That night we could hear the bloodhounds because they had tracked the prisoners to our area. Normally I would have gone to the church on Saturday night, but I said, "Joyce, rather than going down on Saturday, I'm going to stay here with you tonight. Then I'll get up real early Sunday morning in time to get to church." That night we could hear the activity around us as they were trying to track those killers in our vicinity.

Early in the morning I got up to get ready. Our little trailer did not have a bathroom in it. There was a community washhouse in the park. I got my things together to go over there to bathe and shave and get ready to go. It was gray dawn.

I looked behind a trailer and I saw a convict. There was no doubt that he was a prisoner because he had on convict clothes. There was nobody else out there to help. I didn't want to get engaged with some killer convict, but I didn't want to run. I didn't want to scream because this would alarm him. And, I didn't know what he might do. I thought, *Surprise is the best weapon.* So I decided I would pounce him.

Now you have to understand that I was on a football scholarship at the time. I was in pretty good shape. I had the drop on him. Normally, common sense would have told me to run and get out of there. Had I done that, I would have left Joyce alone a few doors away. So I began to move closer and closer around the trailer, and then I jumped him. I got him around the neck and I put him on my hip, did a hammer lock on him, and put him down.

He began to yell and squeal and say, "Let me go. I'm not one of them." I said, "Yes, you are." He said, "I am not." I said, "I see your uniform. I know who you are." About that time a sheriff's deputy came around with a dog. He said, "Mister, you can let him go. He's working with us." At that moment, I prayed, "Thank you, Lord!"

Why on earth would I jump a man like that—a man whom I thought was a killer? I tell you one reason. There was a girl I loved several doors away, and God gave me a protective instinct. Today I'm not the man I used to be, but if you put your hand on my wife or one of my kids, and if I can, I'll put you on the ground. You don't touch a man's children. You don't touch a man's wife. God wants us to have a protective instinct. The man is to be the protector. He's to be the provider.

Recently, James Dobson concluded his program with these words: "I beg you to defend your children. If you won't defend your kids, who will you defend? What are you willing to fight for if it is not your children?" You need to protect your home because there is great danger out there. There is a killer on the loose. John 10:10 says, "The thief does not come except to steal, and to kill, and to destroy." There is a thief, a murderer, a destroyer, and he's loose in your city. He's in your neighborhood. He may be in your living room. And your protective instincts need to say, "I'm going to do something about it."

It's time for some courage!

The Big Lie

Actually, snakes causing problems in the home are nothing new. The original scaly serpent, Satan himself, slithered his way into the Garden of Eden, and he's been destroying homes ever since. Satan's *modus operandi* is the lie, and pornography is perhaps his biggest lie of all.

In his plan to deceive, the devil has substituted all kinds of sources of authority for God's truth. Let me mention some of them.

First, there is *relativism*. Everything is relative. There's no fixed standard of right and wrong.

There was once a philosopher, a brilliant man whose name was Hegel. He had this idea that everything is in flux. He said, over here is an idea. We'll call that idea a postulate or a thesis. Over here, he said, is an opposing idea—an antithesis. Neither one of them may

∾

There is a thief, a murderer, a destroyer, and he's loose in your city. He's in your neighborhood. He may be in your living room. And your protective instincts need to say, "I'm going to do something about it."

∾

really be true, but people believe them—some the thesis, and others the antithesis. So there's a war between this thesis and this antithesis. These fight and these battle. And after a while there comes something called a synthesis. The two ideas come together to make a third idea.

For example, let's give you an illustration that perhaps you can understand. Let's say that the thesis is capitalism. Let's say that the antithesis is Communism. And let's say these get in a battle long enough and you come together with a synthesis, which is what? Socialism. Now that synthesis becomes a new thesis. And then somebody else gets another antithesis. And the new thesis and the antithesis go to war and then you come up with a new synthesis.

Do you see what's happening? Everything is moving. There is no fixed, solid standard. And so all these non-biblical ideas just chase other ideas across the terrain. Yesterday's porn is today's adult entertainment.

In his book, *The Closing of the American Mind*, noted author Allan Bloom said:

> There is one thing a professor can be absolutely certain of: almost every student entering the university believes, or says he believes, that truth is relative . . .
>
> Some are religious, some atheists; some to the Left, some

to the Right; some intend to be scientists, some human-
ists or professionals or businessmen; some are poor, some
rich. They are unified only in their relativism and in the
allegiance to equality . . . The students, of course, cannot
defend their opinion. It is something with which they
have been indoctrinated. The best they can do is point
out all the opinions and cultures there are and have been.
What right, they ask, do I or anyone else have to say one
is better than the others?[2]

Other people are living by *subjectivism*. What is subjectivism?

"Well, I just feel this is right."

"I just feel this is wrong."

"I don't feel porn is so bad, so it must be okay."

So everything is based on feeling. And our young people are
being taught, "Be true to your feelings."

Another substitute for fixed truth is *rationalism*. People say,
"No, don't live by your feelings. Live by your mind. Figure it out.
Weigh it. Test it. Put it in a test tube. Pull out your slide rule. Get
out your calculator and figure it out." Behavior is based on logic.
"Thus saith the mind of man" rather than "thus saith the Word of
God."

For others, the way may be *pragmatism*. Some people don't even
ask, "Is it true?" any more. They just ask, "Does it work?" Ours is
a very pragmatic society.

But we've come today to the worst condition of all, which is
postmodernism.

Now I know that you are not necessarily turned on by that
word. I know that you didn't read this far saying, "I hope he will

mention post-modernism. I've just been salivating thinking about post-modernism."

What is postmodernism? Modernism tried to determine what is right or wrong, and the liberals and the conservatives argued. But postmodernists don't argue about it because they say there is no fixed truth. There is no right. There is no wrong. They ask, "Is there any truth at all?" This leads to the creation of your own so-called "truth." Speak about moral standards, and the postmodernist calls you judgmental. He might say to you, "Now listen, what's true for you may not be true for me. What's true for me may not be true for you."

You want your children to live right? You want your children to do right? Parents, you had better inculcate in their hearts and in their minds that there is a fixed standard of truth and it is the Word of God. If you don't, you are fighting a battle that you are going to lose. In today's society, it is not enough for you to put your hands on your hips and say, "That is wrong." "Why, Daddy?" "Don't ask me why. It's wrong because I said so."

That won't work. If you say, "Just because I say so," you're going to fail. You need to say, "Son, it is wrong to steal because God said so. It is wrong to commit adultery because God says so. You are to obey your parents because God says so. You're to have a clean thought life because God says so." You are to put some rock-ribbed convictions into the hearts of your children.

What is my job as a dad? What is my job as a grandfather? What is your duty, your job? The apostle John said, "I have no greater joy than to hear that my children walk in truth" (3 John 4). I can say "Amen" to that! I have no greater joy than to hear my children walk in truth. You see, it is the truth that sets you free.

Jesus prayed this for us in John 17:17 (KJV): "Sanctify them through thy truth: thy word is truth." The Phillips translation gives it this way: "Make them holy by the truth." Do you want holy children? They are going to have to know the truth.

Can you understand why there is such a battle against the idea of an inspired Bible and a fixed standard of right and wrong? Satan's first words to Eve were, "Has God said . . .?" This is where it starts—doubt, then deception, then disobedience, and then defilement.

In the place of relativism, subjectivism, rationalism, pragmatism, and postmodernism, how about some good old-fashioned "mom-and-dadism"? How about some parents with backbone who will not give up or cave in? Parents who point their kids to the Word of God.

Along with that backbone, let's mix in a generous amount of common sense. Let's take some action and nail up the snake holes that have let the vipers in.

In the following chapters we will give some practical ways to do just that.

Endnotes

1. *Memphis Commercial Appeal*, March 8, 2002. Compiled by Kevin McDaniel from these news services: Associated Press, Los Angeles Times/Washington Post, The New York Times, and Scripps Howard.
2. Allan Bloom, *The Closing of the American Mind* (New York: Simon and Schuster, 1987), 25–26.

∽ 4 ∽

Trash or Treasure?

Helping Your Kids Say No to Pornography

Is it practical to think that we can eliminate pornography? Can we legislate it out of existence? What is the solution to the pornography problem?

The answer is not in *political action.* Though we ought to do all we can do politically, the solution is not ultimately there. The problem is too pervasive.

The answer is not through *electronic safeguards.* Later on in this book, there is some information about some firewalls, some electronic safeguards. But all of these can be overridden by children who outsmart adult supervision.

Warnings are not enough because the pull and the enticement and the curiosity of pornography are too strong. There can be no ultimate victory over pornography until you first learn to choose wisely and teach your children to choose wisely. We're going to have to take the policeman off the street corner and put him in the heart.

It Takes Something Better

Would you, as a parent, like to have a formula, an action plan that you can share with your children that will enable them to say *no* to pornography? If I could show you such a plan, would you be interested? In this chapter, I want to give you a three-step action plan and then show you how to apply it with your kids.

First, I want to give you a principle that these three steps are based upon: *It takes something better to give up something bad.* You will never be able to teach your kids to refuse trash until you first teach them to choose treasure. Too many of us are telling our children, "Don't do this, don't look at that, that's bad for you." If that is your approach, I've got news for you—you're fighting a losing battle. To get them to not go after the bad, you've got to show them something better. I call this the Meat-Bone Principle, based on the following illustration.

The Meat-Bone Principle

Did you ever try to take a nasty bone away from a dog? It's a good way to get bitten. But I'll tell you how to get a bone away from a dog. Put a steak on the ground! The dog will look at that steak and think about what he's got in his mouth.

Now what will he do? He'll go through a process. Step number one, *musing*—steak or bone? Step number two, *choosing*—he thinks to himself, "I'd rather have the steak." Step number three, *refusing*—he spits out the dirty bone. Even a dog has got that much sense. First he evaluates. Then he chooses, and then he refuses. You are not going to lead your children until you take the same steps. They make a proper evaluation. Then they make a clear choice. And then they make a refusal. And they'll say, "No, that nasty bone is not for me."

This is the same three-step process we need to use to help our kids to say *no* to pornography, and we find all three steps by studying the life of Moses.

Learn to Think Like Moses

From the time he was a child, Moses was raised by Pharaoh in Pharaoh's court. When Moses came of age, he was standing in line for the throne. He was to be the king of Egypt, the Pharaoh. He had at his fingertips pleasure, power, position—anything he wanted. But of course, Egypt was ungodly, wicked, lascivious, and he would have been a part of that. He would have had so much. But he would have lost so much.

Holy Moses!

However, Moses made a choice. He said, "I refuse to be the king of Egypt." Hebrews 11:24–26 says, "By faith Moses, when he became of age, refused to be called the son of Pharaoh's daughter, choosing rather to suffer affliction with the people of God than to enjoy the passing pleasures of sin, esteeming the reproach of Christ greater riches than the treasures in Egypt; for he looked to the reward."

∽

You will never be able to teach your kids to refuse trash until you first teach them to choose treasure.

∽

Moses had to choose between the pleasures of sin and the reproach of Christ. Moses saw these two, and he chose Christ and refused Egypt. Now, why did he do that? Hebrews 11:26 says, "For he looked to the reward." Moses looked beyond immediate gratification and by faith chose something of far more lasting value.

He took the same three steps I have mentioned:

He evaluated ("esteeming . . . the riches of Christ").

He chose ("choosing rather").

He refused ("refused to be called the son of Pharaoh's daughter").

You've Got to Choose

Just like Moses chose, you have to make a choice, and every member of your family has to make a choice. There will not be victory in your family; there will be no victory with your children until they make a choice. I cannot say this strongly enough—there must be a choice.

Like Moses, you choose by faith. How do you have faith? You have to hear from God. The Bible tells us in Romans 10:17 that "faith comes by hearing, and hearing by the word of God." Make no mistake about it. Moses had heard from God. And once Moses heard from God, he was able to make a choice.

Satan's strategy is to keep your children from hearing from God. If your children do not hear from God, they cannot make a faith choice. And if your children do not make a faith choice, they're going to go down. They are going to fail. Because it is the Word of God that gets in their hearts, enabling them to overcome evil by choosing what is right.

Remember, Satan's chief weapon is to steal away the Word of God from the hearts and minds of young people. If you do not have a word from God, you will have little hope—whether you are a teenager or an adult—of overcoming pornography.

As parents, you need to help your children follow the same three-step process that Moses used to make the correct choice. Let's look at the first step in the process.

1. Learn to Discern Trash from Treasure

There must be a wise evaluation. Now, Satan does not want you to make that wise evaluation. He doesn't want your children to discern. He doesn't want them to see that his "treasures" are actually trash.

You need to help your children choose God's treasure and refuse Satan's trash, like Moses did. But before they are able to evaluate properly, there must be a system of true values in place.

According to the Meat-Bone Principle, a dog will refuse a nasty bone if offered a T-bone steak. What if we offered the dog something more valuable than the steak? Let's say, a library full of rare first editions—Chaucer, Milton, Dickens, Shakespeare. How about a collection of original paintings by the masters—Renoir, Van Gogh, Picasso? Perhaps a vault full of precious gems—emeralds, rubies, diamonds.

What would he do? He would choose the bone. Why? Because a dog does not have the ability to discern true and lasting values. He is more concerned with immediate gratification.

This is how Satan lures your kids with pornography. He gets them to believe the lie that the pleasure of immediate gratification is worth more than true treasure.

If he cannot get them to believe a lie outright, he will try to confuse them with gradually changing standards.

The Russian psychologist Pavlov did some experiments with a dog. Pavlov trained the dog to jump to the left when he saw a circle on the ground. The dog continued to do this. Then Pavlov trained the dog to jump to the right when he saw an oval on the ground. The dog learned this, too.

Then Pavlov began to gradually distort the circle into an oval until the dog could not discern whether it was a circle or an oval. The dog went mad.

Kids today have similar problems discerning right from wrong without a fixed standard. Satan is a master of distortion.

Conventional wisdom says what our society needs is more information, more communication, and more instruction. This is the premise of the sex education movement, now decades old.

The idea is that if you inform the kids, they will make better decisions. Careful study and observation prove these assumptions are wrong. It is a flawed premise.

Far more powerful than what people know is what they value—their sense of good and bad, treasure and trash. These values come from the Word of God and significant people who are respected and trusted and who hold the same values. This is where godly parents are so vital.

Ask yourself this question: "What are the lasting treasures I would like to write on my children's hearts? What are some eternal values I would like them to embrace?" I'd like to give you three of these values—three treasures—that are worth far more than any of the pleasures of sin.

The Treasure of Fellowship with God. Your children need to understand how great it is to have a clean heart that brings fellowship with God. Jesus said in Matthew 5:8, "Blessed are the pure in heart, for they shall see God." Pornography will blur the vision of God. A clean heart is its own reward—fellowship with God. When the heart is pure, God is real. And then we can have that incredible fellowship with God.

In I John 1:3–4, John says, "That which we have seen and heard we declare to you, that you also may have fellowship with us; and truly our fellowship is with the Father and with His Son Jesus Christ. And these things we write to you that your joy may be full."

Do you want fullness of joy? Then have fellowship with one another and with Jesus Christ. "This is the message which we have heard from Him and declare to you, that God is light and in Him is no darkness at all. If we say that we have fellowship with Him, and walk in darkness, we lie and do not practice the truth:

But if we walk in the light as He is in the light, we have fellowship with one another, and the blood of Jesus Christ His Son cleanses us from all sin" (1 John 1:5–7).

I can tell you that a clean heart, a pure heart, is the only kind of heart that can have fellowship with God. And no pornography on earth is worth forfeiting fellowship with God. What a treasure—to have fellowship with God! It makes no difference who you are; if you're into pornography, your fellowship with God is broken. You're in darkness, and you have no joy. If you are into pornography, I can tell you without stutter, stammer, or apology that you are not having fellowship with God. And I can also tell you plainly that you have no joy. There is no pleasure or treasure I would choose over fellowship with God and the joy that comes with it.

Not only do we need to teach our children the treasure of fellowship with God, but we need to teach them the treasure of true love.

The Treasure of True Love. Only a clean heart can truly love. First John 2:15–16 says, "Do not love the world or the things in the world. If anyone loves the world, the love of the Father is not in him. For all that is in the world—the lust of the flesh, the lust of the eyes, and the pride of life—is not of the Father but is of the world." If you get pornography in your life, if your children get pornography in their lives, you and they will automatically lose the ability to love.

When a person has fellowship with God, by the very nature of that fellowship with God, he has the ability to love with godly love. There is nothing more debilitating, nothing more stultifying, nothing more harmful to the ability to love than pornography.

God wants you to love. But pornography is not based on love. It destroys love. It is based on lust.

The greatest gift is love. The greatest ability is the ability to love. If you have everything but love, you have nothing. If you have love, you have everything. No face is as beautiful as the face of the person who is loved.

What good is it to have the treasures of Egypt and have no one you love to share them with? Money, fame, fun, and pleasure are empty without love.

The highest good is to love. The first and great commandment is to love God with all our being and our neighbor as ourselves. The great joy is to love. We have a generation today that talks about making love, but they don't know the difference between love and lust.

A man may say, "I love oranges. They're so good. They're so sweet. I just love oranges." He cuts out a plug, squeezes out the juice, and throws it away. A boy says to a girl, "I just love you. You are so sweet." He doesn't really love her. He loves her like a man loves oranges. All he wants to do is to enjoy all the goodness, the sweetness, the purity, and then throw her away like a piece of garbage.

What's the difference between love and lust? Lust wants to get. Love wants to give. Pornography is based on lust. It looks at people as though people are objects to be used to gratify one's selfishness. When a person feeds on pornography, he has no respect for himself. And it follows as night follows day that he can have no respect for other people. No person who puts garbage in his mind, in his body, has any respect for himself. And if a person has no respect for himself or herself, how do you expect him or her to have respect for other people?

Love is a grand and powerful force that is far more than emotionalism, much less lust. C. S. Lewis has pointed out in *Mere Christianity* the difference between loving and "being in love":

Being in love is a good thing, but it is not the best thing. There are many things below it, but there are also things above it. You cannot make it the basis of a whole life. It is a noble feeling, but it is still a feeling . . . who could bear to live in that excitement for even five years . . . But of course, ceasing to be "in love" need not mean ceasing to love. Love in a second sense—love as distinct from being in love is not merely a feeling.

It is a deep unity, maintained by the will and deliberately strengthened by habits; reinforced by the grace which both parents ask and receive from God.

They can have this love for each other even at those moments when they do not like each other; as you love yourself even when you do not like yourself.

They can retain this love even when each would easily, if they allowed themselves, to be "in love" with someone else. Being "in love" first moved them to promise fidelity; this quieter love enables them to keep the promise. It is on this love that the engine of marriage is run; being "in love" was the explosion that started it.

The Bible says we're to love others as we love ourselves. Do you think it's wrong to love yourself? No. It's right and proper to love yourself. How can I love you as I love me unless I love me? And I'm not talking about standing in front of the mirror and singing,

"How Great Thou Art." If you do that, you're sick. I'm saying that you ought to have some self-respect. You ought to have some love for yourself. And when you have love for yourself, then you will have love for others. Because you're going to want others treated as you want to be treated.

People who are into pornography, especially if they are men, look upon women as if they are objects for their own personal gratification, and they have no absolute love for them. They cannot have love for them because they don't have fellowship with God. How can they then have fellowship with anyone else?

Put it down big, put it down plain, put it down straight: People who treat sex lightly will treat other people lightly. They have no respect for other people. They have a disdainful, trivial, and selfish attitude toward other people.

Don't tell me that pornography is a private act. Don't tell me that pornography is a personal choice. Don't tell me that pornography is a victimless crime. Don't tell me that pornography is harmless entertainment. Put your daughter, your granddaughter out there as the object of some man's lust. Think of your daughter. Think of your granddaughter. That object of lust is somebody's daughter. That person is somebody made in the image of God.

Porn kills the ability to love. It treats people as things. The statistics that I've read are frightening. One out of every four little baby girls will be sexually assaulted some time in her life. One out of four! One out of ten little boys will be sexually assaulted by a male in his lifetime—most of them before they are physically mature. Now, not all people who read pornography do that. A trained policeman said, "Not everyone who reads pornography is a sex deviant. But every sex deviant reads it."

The deviate has little real love for God, himself, or others. Every porn addict is emotionally crippled and cannot fully love. What a great loss it is to lose the ability to love.

The Treasure of a Godly Family. The third treasure you should teach your children to embrace is the treasure of a godly family. Fellowship with God gives us the ability to love. And the ability to love enables us to have a family. God made the family before he made the government, before he made education, before he made the church. The family is the only part of the Garden of Eden that we have left. That's the reason the devil has leveled all of the artillery of hell against the family. Nothing is more devastating to the family than pornography.

You know what I want for my little children, my grandchildren? I want them to have the kind of home my wife Joyce and I have. I want them to enjoy what I have enjoyed. Nothing would move me to sadness and anger more than to feel that somebody had ripped that away from them. A loving, physical bond between husband and wife is God's great and wonderful gift.

Do you think God is opposed to the idea of sex? God created sex. It's God's idea. When God says not to look upon a woman to lust after her, when God says, "Flee fornication," when God says, "Thou shalt not commit adultery," God is not trying to keep sex *from* us. He's keeping sex *for* us. It's God's great gift.

Put it down big, put it down plain, put it down straight: People who treat sex lightly will treat others lightly. They have no respect for other people.

I feel so sorry for young people today. Kids today talk about "going all the way." That is the one thing they do *not* do! You go all the way when you give yourself to somebody heart, body, and soul in a happy marriage. That is going all the way. Many young people today don't know the difference between love and lust, and they miss the best.

I like to put it this way: "If you eat your cake now, you'll have a crummy tomorrow." Pity the Hugh Hefners of this world. Pity the movie starlets with faces like angels and morals like alley cats. Don't let this miserable crowd set the agenda for our kids.

Help your children learn to make a wise evaluation. Help them see that Satan's pleasures are temporary, but God's treasures are eternal. What are the treasures? They are so simple: The treasure of *fellowship with God,* the treasure of *true love,* and the treasure of a *godly home.*

2. SAY YES TO GOD'S RICHES

We must teach our children to choose to say *yes* to God's riches. Once the values are determined, then the choice becomes clear. They will be able to see the difference between treasure and trash, diamonds and dirt.

This doesn't mean that there will be no temptation. There's pleasure in sin; there's pleasure in pornography. Somebody will say, "You're just an old fool if you say there's no pleasure in pornography. I enjoy it." Of course, people enjoy it. The devil's too smart to go fishing without any bait on his hook. But the pleasures of sin are "for a season" (Heb. 11:25 KJV). "Bread gained by deceit is sweet to a man, but afterward his mouth will be filled with gravel" (Prov. 20:17). The Bible is a very straightforward book; it speaks of the pleasures of sin. But it says Moses "chose." It was his values that determined his choice.

There were temptations for Moses. There were the sensual pleasures of Egypt. And every man who has any hormones in him, every teen who has any curiosity—there's a pull toward pornography. Every person who is normal in his or her physiological makeup will feel this pull. Moses, I'm sure, felt a pull toward Egypt.

Moses had been doing some figuring. The Bible says he esteemed the riches of Christ. The word *esteemed* means that he accounted. Moses looked one way and he said, "All right. There are the pleasures, the treasures of Egypt." Then he looked the other way and said, "There are the riches of Christ." Moses saw that which was visible, and he saw that which was invisible. He chose the invisible and the eternal. He said,

If you don't choose, you're going to fail. Nobody is going to drift into purity in these days any more than a boat just drifts into the harbor. You're going to have to choose.

"That's the way I'm going." He chose. Now if you don't make that choice, you're going to fail.

You must choose. Think with me about how choice works. First of all, you're free to choose. Second, you're not free *not* to choose. You say, "Well, I won't choose." You just chose not to choose, which is a choice.

Third, you're not free to choose the consequences of your choice. To reiterate: You're free to choose; you're not free *not* to choose; you are not free to choose the consequences of your choice.

You choose, and then your choice chooses for you. You can choose to jump out of a ten-story window, but then your choice chooses for you, and the law of gravity takes over.[1]

Teach your kids the value of making the right choice, of saying *yes* to God's riches. It was not easy for Moses. It won't be easy for your kids. Parents, it will not be easy for you. And that's the reason you have to make a radical, dramatic, clear choice. Because if you don't choose, you're going to fail. Nobody is going to drift into purity in these days any more than a boat just drifts into the harbor. You're going to have to choose. I cannot say this strongly enough.

3. SAY *NO* TO SATAN'S LIES

In Hebrews 11:24 the Bible says that Moses "refused to be called the son of Pharaoh's daughter." There is both a choosing and a refusing. Moses knew that he couldn't have treasure and trash. He couldn't have both Egypt and the riches of Christ. A lot of people try to, but it can't be done. The Bible says, "A double minded man is unstable in all his ways" (James 1:8 KJV). You just have to say, "When I choose what is right, I must, as night follows day, refuse what is wrong." No one will refuse pornography until he chooses righteousness. And few will choose righteousness until they see the pay off; they evaluate the reward; they see what is there for them.

Remember the dog and the Meat-Bone Principle? It takes something better to give up something bad. You're not going to help your kids do away with pornography until first of all they see the steak. And the steak is a clean heart—fellowship with God, the ability to love and be loved—and the steak is the potentiality for a godly family—the highest good on this earth. Your children have to see that, and they have to believe it.

What do you do to help your children refuse pornography? Show them something better—a clean heart, true love, a godly family. With God's help, teach your kids to discover true values, to discern trash from treasure; to say *yes* to God's best, and *no* to the devil's nasty bones. Once the choice is made, it must be maintained. The next chapter will give some vital help.

Endnotes

1. Adrian Rogers, *What Every Christian Ought to Know* (Broadman & Holman, 2005).

Staying Clean in a Dirty World:

How to Have a Pure Thought Life

If Satan can control your thought life, he has you on a string. Think of these verses:

"Keep your heart with all diligence, for out of it spring the issues of life" (Prov. 4:23).

"For as he thinks in his heart, so is he" (Prov. 23:7).

"For to be carnally minded is death, but to be spiritually minded is life and peace. Because the carnal mind is enmity against God; for it is not subject to the law of God, nor indeed can be. So then, those who are in the flesh cannot please God" (Rom. 8:6–8).

"And you, who once were alienated and enemies in your mind by wicked works, yet now He has reconciled" (Col. 1:21).

The thought is the father of the deed. Yet few people are aware of the danger of a mind out of control.

A newspaper article told about the keepers of Sea World in Orlando. When they opened up the park, there in the pool with the killer whale Tillikum was the body of Daniel Dukes. Evidently, this young man had stayed in the park. After the park closed he decided he would go swimming with the whales. In that pool was an eleven-thousand-pound whale named Tillikum, who was playing with the lifeless body of that young man. Evidently Dukes thought that he could have a good time just swimming with the whales. Our young men and women today are being destroyed by a monster more dangerous than that black and white orca.

So great, so big, so massive is the problem—and yet sometimes so seemingly small. Not all predators weigh eleven thousand pounds. There is a marine parasite very small, almost invisible, that feeds on the shell of a clam and paralyzes the muscle of that clam so it cannot stay shut. Then that tiny parasite goes on the inside and begins to feed on the clam.

Whether a killer whale or whether a tiny parasite feeding on the mind, our boys and girls today are in greater danger than boys and girls on the wild frontier many days ago. There is danger everywhere. We need to do something about it because Satan wants to corrupt their minds.

A Clean Thought Life—Guaranteed!

The Bible has so much to say about the mind. Sometimes in the Old Testament it's called the heart. Proverbs 4:23 says, "Keep your heart with all diligence, for out of it spring the issues of life." Proverbs 23:7 says, "As he thinks in his heart, so is he." Let's state it this way: "You're not what you think you are. But what you think—you are."

Throughout the years, people have done all kinds of things to see if they can correct the thought life. They have searched in caves. They have walked in deserts. They have gone to remote islands. They have lived in the jungles. They have climbed mountains. They have tied themselves up in dungeons. They have lived as hermits. But they have not been able to control the thought life.

A school boy was asked to complete this proverb: "Cleanliness is next to _____." His response was "Cleanliness is next to impossible."

But there is a way. I guarantee you beyond any shadow of a doubt that if you will do what the following verses tell you to do, you will guard your heart. And if you guard your heart, then you are prepared to protect your home.

How can a young man cleanse his way? By taking
heed according to Your word. With my whole heart
I have sought You; oh, let me not wander from Your
commandments! Your word I have hidden in my heart,
that I might not sin against You. Blessed are You,
O LORD! Teach me Your statues. With my lips I have
declared all the judgments of Your mouth. I have rejoiced
in the way of Your testimonies, as much as in all riches.
I will meditate on Your precepts, and contemplate Your

ways. I will delight myself in Your statutes; I will not forget Your word (Ps. 119:9–16).

Comprised in verses 9–16 are seven steps. I will make you this guarantee: If you do the seven things that are listed here, you will, by God's grace, for his glory and your good, control your thought life. But, if you don't do these things, no matter how well your intentions, you have no sure defense. Your mind is like the guidance program in a missile. Show me what you think, and I'll tell you where you are headed.

Let's examine these seven principles.

1. Purification: Start with a Good Bath

"How can a young man cleanse his way? By taking heed according to Your word" (Ps. 119:9).

Principle number one is purification. Get perfectly clean. You must start here.

In Psalm 119:9, the Hebrew word used for "way" has the idea of a rut, a groove. It's something like a groove in a road. A farmer may drive his tractor back and forth over a farm road until there is a rut in that road, a muddy rut. From then on he can just set the tractor and let go of the wheel and the tractor will follow that way.

A Dirt-Track Mind

What the devil has done to so many people is this: He has put a groove, a muddy rut, a dirty track in their minds. They have what I might call a one-track mind. Have you ever been around people that no matter what you say, they're going to make something suggestive out of it? They're going to make some wise crack. Why? Because these people have a rut in their mind. Often lying in bed

> *If all God were to do is to forgive you and not cleanse you, then that would not be enough. Because the problem would still be on the inside.*

when the lights are out and they are alone with their thoughts, ungodly episodes are feature events in the theater of the mind.

The Bible speaks of people like that in Jeremiah 11:8 (KJV): "Yet they obeyed not, nor inclined their ear, but walked every one in the imagination of their evil heart." The imagination of their evil heart— that's what we would call a dirty mind. What they need is a good mind bath—brainwashing in the good sense.

How can the mind be cleansed? Look again: "How can a young man cleanse his way?" The biblical writer asks the question and then he answers it. "By taking heed according to Your word." The Word of God will cleanse and purify your mind (Ps. 119:9).

Jesus said, in John 15:3 (KJV), "Ye are clean through the word which I have spoken unto you." The word he used that is translated "clean" is the Greek word that we get our English word "catharsis" from—*katharsimos*. You have a catharsis, an inward cleansing through the Word of God. The Bible, for example, speaks of the "washing of water by the word" (Eph. 5:26). The Word of God has the ability to cleanse your mind and give a fresh new start.

ROTTEN *FROM* THE CORE

It is so vital that we have a cleansed mind. If you see a worm hole in an apple, this doesn't mean there is a worm in the apple. It means there *was* a worm there. The worm did not eat his way in. He ate his way out. How did he get in? He was born in the heart of the apple. The egg was laid in the blossom. The worm subsequently ate his way to the surface.

The vile thoughts and appetites that we have proceed from an unclean heart. "For out of the heart proceed evil thoughts" (Matt. 15:19). This is why the dirty heart must be cleansed.

CLEAN UP YOUR ACT

Think of the Lord Jesus Christ coming into your mind and doing spring housecleaning. Think of him just cleaning out everything in your mind that is not what it ought to be. That is exactly what he is able to do. The Bible says in I John 1:9, "If we confess our sins, He is faithful and just to forgive us our sins and to *cleanse* us from all unrighteousness" (emphasis added). You want some good news? No matter what your thought life has been, no matter how vile, no matter how obscene, you can be as clean and as pure as the driven snow.

If all God were to do is to forgive you and not cleanse you, then that would not be enough. Because the problem would still be on the inside. Forgiveness is good, but cleansing goes beyond forgiveness. If you stole ten dollars from me and came back and said, "I want to pay you back. I stole this ten dollars. Will you forgive me?" I could forgive you, but I couldn't cleanse you. God not only forgives, but he cleanses.

That's the promise we have in this verse. If God did not forgive you and God did not cleanse you, according to his own Word, God would be unfaithful and God would be unjust. God would be a liar and a criminal.

YOU'RE RIGHT; I'M WRONG

Let's examine the word *confess* in I John 1:9. It's a Greek word, *homologōmen.* It's a combination of two words that literally mean "to say the same." It doesn't mean to admit our sins. You could admit your sin, but that wouldn't be a Bible confession. It might be a confession in a courtroom, but not according to the Bible.

It is not merely saying, "I have done something wrong." To confess means that you say, "I agree with you, God. I come over and take sides against this sin. I say with you, dear God, that I've done it and it is wrong. And I say with you, God, what you say about that sin. It is lust, filthiness, and dirt. I make no excuses." That is a confession. Once you make that confession, God is faithful and just to forgive you and to cleanse you.

If you would have victory, that's the very first step. You're going to have to get your mind clean. And there's no reason you cannot do that. You can get your mind perfectly clean—not just from the sin of wrong thinking, but any sinful thing that may be there. Because if there is any sin there—any whatsoever—that is unconfessed and unrepented, you're not going to have victory. If you don't have victory in one area, you cannot claim it in another area. You can't have segmented victory.

WHITE CORNERS

I used to pastor a little country church in a town called Fellsmere, and there was a sugar mill out by town. I was a college student when I pastored that church, and I would go out there and visit the men in my church who worked at the sugar mill.

They had a big garage where they fixed the tractors and other equipment. One of the members of my church ran that big garage machine shop. You wouldn't think that a machine shop could be that clean. The floors were clean and slick. There was no trash lying around. There was no grease. Everything was clean. The tools were all put up in a certain place. I stood in awe of how clean and neat this shop was.

If you're halfhearted about a clean thought life in this X-rated society, you will never have victory. You're going to have to say, "With every inch, every ounce, every nerve, every fiber, every sinew, O God, with my whole heart, I will seek You."

Then I noticed something unusual. That man had painted every corner of that machine shop white. I asked him about it. I said, "Why are the corners white?" He replied, "I found out if you keep the corners white you can keep the rest of the shop clean." He wouldn't allow anybody to put anything in a corner. Every corner was white. I thought, *That's what I need to do—keep the corners of my mind clean.* Don't just try to clean up the main part. Keep it all perfectly clean.

2. Determination: A Wholehearted Commitment

"With my whole heart I have sought You; oh, let me not wander from Your commandments" (Ps. 119:10).

The second principle is the principle of *determination*. It's not enough to get clean, because you'll get defiled again if you don't determine to stay clean. Some people will never have victory over their thought life because they are halfhearted rather than wholehearted. No one has ever won a moral victory halfheartedly.

If you're halfhearted about a clean thought life in this X-rated society, you will not have victory. You're going to have to say, "With every inch, every ounce, every nerve, every fiber, every sinew, O God, with my whole heart, I will seek You." If you don't do that, you're not going to make it. It takes determination.

Here are some other verses that speak about determination:

But from there you will seek the LORD your God, and you will find Him if you seek Him with all your heart and with all your soul (Deut. 4:29).

A double minded man is unstable in all his ways (James 1:8 KJV).

Draw near to God and He will draw near to you. Cleanse your hands, you sinners; and purify your hearts, you double-minded (James 4:8).

But Daniel purposed in his heart that he would not defile himself (Dan. 1:8).

Job said in Job 31:1 (KJV), "I made a covenant with mine eyes; why then should I look upon a maid?" (The Hebrew idea is that I will not lust after a woman.)

Question: Have you done that? Have you said, "With all of my heart I determine to be pure." God does business with those who mean business. After you do this, it doesn't mean the battle is over. But it will never be victoriously won until you go to battle with all of your heart. First, *get* perfectly clean. And then say by God's grace, "I will *stay* clean."

Years ago I read how people would hunt for ermine—a little animal from which fur coats were made. This particular ermine had a snow white coat. They would find the hole where the ermine would hide. And they would smear filth around the hole—something vile, dirty, and defiling. Then the dogs would hunt the ermine, and the ermine would run as fast as he could to the hole.

But when the ermine saw that filth, it would turn around and face the dogs. It would *give its life* rather than defile itself.

> ∽
>
> *The Word of God hidden in your heart will fortify you. But it has to be in your heart, not in your dresser drawer.*
>
> ∽

Does purity mean that much to you? If not, you are half-hearted. And if you're halfhearted, you're not going to make it.

3. Fortification: God's Word In . . . Garbage Out

"Your word I have hidden in my heart, that I might not sin against You" (Ps. 119:11).

You've probably heard the axiom that computer programmers use: "Garbage In . . . Garbage Out." Well, I have some great news for you: As soon as the Word of God goes in, garbage goes out! You need to fortify yourself daily with the Word of God. Yes, you can get clean. Yes, you can be determined. But you need more than that. You need something to fortify you on the inside. You need to be fortified by the Word of God.

First you *repent* and get clean. And then you *refuse* to participate. But next, after repentance and refusal comes *replacement*. You put something there in the place of that which you have refused and that which God has taken out. It is like recording over a used tape. Nature abhors a vacuum. The Word of God hidden in your heart will fortify you. But it has to be in your heart, not in a dresser drawer. Look at verse 11 (KJV) again: "Thy word have I hid in my *heart,* that I might not sin against thee."

HIDE IT IN YOUR HEART

One of the greatest weapons against pornography is the hiding of God's Word in the heart. Scripture reveals the mind of God. When you have Scripture in your heart and mind, you're thinking God's thoughts after him. Casual thoughts, casual reading of the Bible is like a bee just flitting over the surface of a flower. Memorization is like the bee going down into the heart of the flower and gathering the nectar. Meditation is like him taking it back to the hive and making honey out of it. What we need to do is gather the Word of God so we can memorize and meditate on it.

∽

The thought is the dress rehearsal for the deed.

∽

Memory is an incredible thing. I imagine that most of you can remember the first dirty story you ever heard as a child—that first impure thing written upon your mind. The memory is still there. Oliver Wendell Holmes said about the memory, "Memory is a crazy witch. She treasures bits of rags and straw and throws her jewels out the window." So many people remember what they ought to forget and forget what they ought to remember.

Scripture memory helps you to remember what you ought to remember and to forget what you ought to forget. The mind is a marvelous thing. The best computer on earth is an idiot compared to the human mind. A mind can think about itself thinking. It's an incredible thing. A mind filled with Scripture is powerful.

Do you remember what the Bible says in Psalm 119:11? "Your word I have hidden in my heart, that I might not sin against You." When you put the right thing in your mind, it crowds out the wrong thing.

Do you want to teach your children to live victoriously? Teach them to memorize Scripture and reward them for memorizing Scripture. Some say, "Well, I don't believe in bribing kids to do good." It's not a bribe; it's a reward. A bribe is an inducement to do evil. A reward is a recognition for doing good. The Bible teaches the idea of rewards. Reward your children for learning Scripture. It will be one of the best investments you can make.

BOXES OF JUNK

Imagine a beautiful little box made of porcelain. Women like little boxes. My wife likes them. I buy her little decorative boxes every now and then. I want you to imagine a little box with filigrees of gold, platinum, silver, encrusted with gems and diamonds with a beautifully crafted hinge and latch.

When you see that little box, you think, "What a beautiful box that is." Then you open it up and look inside. It contains gem clips, toothpicks, gum wrappers, and rubber bands. The mind is like that—such an incredible instrument. And what do some people put in their minds? Just junk. No wonder they have trashy thoughts.

The thought is the dress rehearsal for the deed. "You sow a thought, you reap a deed. Sow a deed, you reap a habit. Sow a habit you reap a character. Sow a character and you reap a destiny." It all begins with the thought. James Allen said, "Good thoughts bear good fruit. Bad thoughts bear bad fruit. And man is his own gardener."

A Security Check Before Flights of Fancy

You can choose your thoughts like you choose your friends. What you need to do is to put a guard on your mind. If you travel by air as I do, you are familiar with the security checkpoint system in the airport. Before you pass through the metal detector, you must first take off anything that might set off the alarm—your watch, your belt buckle, your cell phone. Then you can pass through.

You need to have a checkpoint like that at the gate of your mind. There are certain things that you just don't let through.

Here's what Paul said: "Finally, brethren, whatsoever things are true, whatsoever things are honest, whatsoever things are just, whatsoever things are pure, whatsoever things are lovely, whatsoever things are of good report; if there be any virtue, and if there be any praise, think on these things. Those things, which ye have both learned, and received, and heard, and seen in me, do: and the God of peace shall be with you" (Phil. 4:8–9 KJV).

In this passage God gives a checklist for the mind. Make every thought pass through this test before it is welcomed.

The reliance test. "Whatsoever things are true." We are not talking about facts, but truth. Our society no longer asks, "Is it true?" but "Does it work?" That is not enough.

The respect test. "Whatsoever things are honest." Honest means honorable or worthy of respect. Don't let dishonorable thoughts in.

The rightness test. "Whatsoever things are just." Just means straight over against that which is crooked. Are you thinking straight?

The reverence test. "Whatsoever things are pure." Pure means free from contamination. It speaks of something that would be used in the worship of God. That is, is it fit for the presence of God?

The relationship test. "Whatsoever things are lovely." Lovely means causing us to love. It is a combination of two words, which mean "toward love." Pornography destroys true love.

The refinement test. "Whatsoever things are of good report." Good report means high-toned. It sounds good. Some say, "I don't know why people always come to me and tell me these things." I know why. They know you will listen. You let them track mud on the carpet of your mind.

Paul then sums up it all up: "If there be any virtue, any praise, think on these things."

> *If you are thinking about what is right, you cannot be thinking about what is wrong.*

A WONDERFUL IMPOSSIBILITY

Let me share with you something wonderful, something glorious. God made you in such a way that you can't think two thoughts at one time. And if you're thinking what is right, you cannot be thinking what is wrong. And the way not to think what is wrong is to think what is right.

You cannot *not* think impure thoughts because while you're trying not to think impure thoughts, you're thinking about the impure thoughts you're trying not to think about. It's a catch-22. It's a vicious trap.

Don't Think About an Elephant

Let's do an experiment. I want you to do your best not to think about an elephant for the next thirty seconds. Whatever you do, don't think about an elephant. Don't think about his trunk, his big floppy ears, or his tusks. Okay, time is up. Now what are you thinking about? You're thinking about the elephant you were trying not to think about. Isn't that right? But you were not thinking about a zebra because you were thinking about an elephant. Right? This is why your mind needs to be saturated with and fortified by the Word of God.

If you're thinking about one thing, you're not thinking about another thing. Because you cannot think two thoughts at one time. If you're thinking about what is right, you cannot be thinking about what is wrong. When you fortify yourself with the Word of God, you're thinking God's thoughts after him.

You say, "But what if I'm watching television, and all of a sudden some suggestive thing comes on? It just bombards my mind. I didn't choose to watch that. What do I do then?"

Same Thing, Only Different

Do you know the difference between carnal people and Spirit-filled people? It is the way they look at these things. They see them from a different viewpoint. Even when a Spirit-filled person is confronted with something like that, they still think about it in the light of God's Word. It is not only a matter of *what* you think about, but also *how* you think about things. The spiritual mind and the carnal mind may think about the same things, but they don't think about the same things the same way.

The spiritual mind discerns it from a different viewpoint. Never willingly bring anything impure into your mind, but when you have to face it, you're still facing it through the lens of God's Word. It can be a teachable moment.

GO ON THE OFFENSIVE

Learn to counterattack. Be not overcome with evil, but overcome evil with good. Now there are ways that you cannot keep these things from happening. You walk through the mall—there it is. You turn on the television—there it is. At the newsstand— there it is. You can't go around with blinders. But you *can* counterattack. The difference between people is not primarily *what* they think about, but *how* they think about what they think about.

Perhaps you are walking along with your son, and there's somebody at a news rack looking through an obscene magazine. What do you do? You use that as a teaching tool. You say, "Son, look at that. What do you think is going through that man's mind right now? What do you think God thinks about that? Have you ever felt that? What do you think God would have us do? Son, can you think of a good Scripture that would help you in a situation like that?"

Do you know what David did? David cut Goliath's head off with Goliath's own sword. You can use these unexpected ambushes against the devil if you're wise enough. Learn how to counterattack and turn it back on the enemy.

4. Evaluation: Remember What Really Counts

"I have rejoiced in the way of Your testimonies, as much as in all riches" (Ps. 119:14).

Remember where the true riches are. If you were to show me a room filled with gold from floor to ceiling, and say, "You can have it all, but you can't have the Word of God," I wouldn't have to even think about it. I would say, "I'll take the Word." That's not rhetoric; I mean that with all my heart.

Suppose I've been feeding on a wonderful meal my wife has cooked for me, and I am filled and satisfied. Then somebody meets me with a plate of stale crumbs, or some food with maggots in it, and says, "Here, eat this." I would say, "No thank you, I'm already satisfied."

When you see what you have in Jesus, you don't have to be in a back alley, eating tin cans with the devil's billy goats. Don't feel sorry for me because I don't watch pornography. Pity the people who do. Remember the chapter on trash or treasure? The pure mind will not trade diamonds for dirt.

5. Vitalization: Let God Make It Live

"Blessed are You, O LORD! Teach me Your statutes" (Ps. 119:12).

Principle number 5 is vitalization. Ask God to teach you. Turn fortification into prayer. Say, "Now, O God, teach me." Pray and ask God to put his mighty hand upon you. Facts and memory are not enough, even Bible facts. You need the presence and power of God.

You cannot separate the Word of God from the God of that Word. And you must pray, "O God, make it real in my heart." The Holy Spirit in you will take the Word of God, which is living and alive and will vitalize it for you.

Bill was a new Christian. He was being mentored and taught the Bible by a man named Charlie. They had great fellowship (and it's always good to have a mentor to teach the Word of God to you). But one day Bill was studying the Scripture and Charlie was nowhere around. He said to himself, "I wonder what that means? Boy, when Charlie comes, I'm going to ask him what that means." Then he felt the Holy Spirit whispering to him, "Why don't you ask me? I'm the one who taught Charlie."

∼

Learn to speak the Word of God, to share the Word of God, and to sing the Word of God.

∼

You can pray and say, "Lord, teach me. Teach me your statutes, your law." Vitalize it. Let God energize you.

A vital prayer life is so important. Psalm 119:12 is a prayer of dependency. Prayerlessness is bad enough, but what prayerlessness indicates is even worse. It indicates that we're quite confident that we can do it by ourselves. We cannot!

First, you hide God's Word in your heart. Then you say, "God, vitalize it. Make it real to me. I don't want to be just rattling off memory verses. Let it be the living Word in me."

6. Verbalization: What You Say Is What You Get

"With my lips have I declared all the judgments of Your mouth" (Ps. 119:13).

The next principle is verbalization. Keep the Word of God on your lips. The psalmist has already spoken about the Word of God in the heart, but now he talks about the Word of God on the lips. Now you begin to verbalize it. Confession and profession are linked together. You take the Word of God and begin to download it to other people. Or just speak it out loud to God.

Sometimes you may sing it. Many of today's praise and worship songs are Bible verses set to music. Singing Scripture is one of the best things you can do to have the Word of God in your mouth, in your lips. Why? Because there is a symbiotic relationship. The Word of God goes from the heart to the mouth out and from the mouth back to the heart, and one builds upon another. Also, as you move in and out among brothers and sisters, you verbalize the Word of God. Both you and they are built up.

Learn to speak the Word of God, to share the Word of God, and to sing the Word of God. Not only do you vitalize it and say, "Lord, teach it to me," but you verbalize it and begin to share it with other people. Just the very speaking of God's Word gives you force for the fight.

We read in the book of the Revelation where the saints were at warfare with Satan: "They overcame him by the blood of the Lamb and by the word of their testimony, and they did not love their lives to the death" (Rev. 12:11). Did you know that you can not only give your testimony to other people; you can give it to yourself? You can say, "I belong to you, Lord Jesus; you're mine." Have you ever given your testimony to yourself? I give mine to me lots of times. I just say who I am in the Lord Jesus Christ. It brings confidence and victory.

7. Meditation: Think on These Things

"I will meditate on Your precepts, and contemplate Your ways. I will delight myself in Your statutes; I will not forget Your word" (Ps. 119:15–16).

The final principle is meditation—maintaining a constant communion with the Lord. Meditation is a powerful force to keep your mind pure.

There are three major elements in meditation: time, quietness, and concentration. If you will spend some time concentrating on the Word of God and thinking about it, it will do something wonderful for your thought life.

The word *meditate* may be compared to a cow chewing the cud. When a cow in the pasture feeds on clover and alfalfa, she must digest it. She has four stomachs, and she places her lunch in one of these. Then she will go out to "meditate." That is, she'll lie down in the pasture somewhere, and the brain sends a message to a stomach and says, "Alfalfa, please." Up comes the alfalfa, and she will chew it again and swallow it down. And then, "Clover, please." She chews that for a while, gets the juice out of it, and sends it back down again.

The Word of God is like that. You get it in your mind, you ingest it, then you digest it. You chew on it over and over and over again. I find myself going to bed thinking the Word of God, waking up in the morning thinking the Word of God.

The Word of God is also like a tune that you can't get out of your mind. You find yourself humming it through the day. You need to get the Word of God into your mind so you can meditate on it day after day.

Let me give you a few verses on meditation in this same psalm:

I will meditate on Your precepts, and contemplate
Your ways (v. 15).

Princes also sit and speak against me, but Your ser-
vant meditates on Your statutes (v, 23).

My hands also I will lift up to Your commandments,
which I love, and I will meditate on Your statutes (v. 48).

Oh, how I love Your law! It is my meditation all the
day (v. 97).

Let's sum it up. All we have mentioned is rooted in the basic passage—Psalm 119:9–16. Here are the seven steps to a clean thought life—guaranteed!

- Purification: Get clean
- Determination: Mean business
- Fortification: Put in the Word of God
- Evaluation: Remember true riches
- Vitalization: Let God teach you
- Verbalization: Speak the Word of God
- Meditation: Think on these Things

It's time to have a checkup from the neck up. How about your mind? Are you serious about staying clean in a dirty world? You can! Don't say it won't work without trying it. It will work—guaranteed!

∾ 6 ∾

Seven Strategies to Snakeproof Your Home

Remember the Nelson family from chapter 3? They are still having snake problems. Not the reptile kind; they finally figured out that they needed to plug the hole where the snakes were coming in. The problems now are with music, videos, and questionable Web sites.

Satan has many ways to invade the sanctity and security of your home.

The Snake's in the Mail

Consider the following news report from the Associated Press:

LITTLE ROCK—A live copperhead is a threatening communication when sent through the mail, according to an indictment from a federal grand jury. The indictment released Thursday accuses a Pocahontas lawyer and his son of mailing the snake Sept. 29 to another man in their hometown.

Bob Sam Castleman and his son, Robert Jerrod Castleman, are charged in the indictment with mailing a threatening communication to Albert Coy Staton.

Kathy Staton opened the package in her pickup truck in front of her home. "It was on my lap when I opened it and the snake popped up and its head was within 2 inches of my face," she said Thursday.

She threw the box down inside the truck, and a passenger grabbed the box and threw it out a window. Staton said the 3-foot snake "was the fattest copperhead I've ever seen."

The indictment said the two Castlemans knowingly sent a package "containing a poisonous reptile, to wit, a live mature copperhead . . . with intent to kill or injure."

We may not receive literal snakes in the mail, but what about "video vipers" with lethal lyrics? Natalie brought home a video from a friend's house. It was a teen comedy—last summer's number one rated draw at theaters across the county. A seemingly harmless film spoofing the horror film genre. Mom wasn't too concerned because she had heard that most of the kids at school and church had seen it.

But, Mom got curious when she picked up the box in Natalie's room and saw that it was rated R—for adult situations, profanity, vulgarity, and nudity.

What the Nelsons need to do is the same thing you need to do: Adopt some strategies to snakeproof your home *and* your heart. Here are seven steps to follow. They are intensely spiritual, yet very practical.

I. Install Software for the Heart

Let's imagine you have a computer that is not functioning properly; it keeps crashing and locking up. Your neighbor, Richard, a self-proclaimed know-it-all stops by to take a look.

He then gives you his "expert" assessment: "Boy, what a pile of antiquity. You must have bought this thing at least twelve months ago! I bet your CD-ROM drive is too slow. You probably need to replace it with one of the new super-fast ones that also let you burn your own CDs and DVDs. You should also buy an optical mouse. They track much more smoothly, *and* you don't even need a mouse pad."

At the computer store, you relay the symptoms to the technician, including Richard's advice. He quickly gives you *his* expert assessment: "You don't have a hardware problem at all. You can buy a new mouse or CD-ROM drive, but that won't keep your computer from crashing. The problem with your computer is your *operating system has become corrupted.* All you need to do is install new software and it should work just fine."

Unfortunately, there are a lot of "Richards" in the world trying to solve behavior problems the same way: working on the externals, while the *real problem is inside.* First of all, before you work at putting any external solutions into place, you need to install *software for the heart.*

Why do we need to start with the heart? The Bible makes it clear. Jeremiah 17:9 tells us, "The heart is deceitful above all things, and desperately wicked." Jesus said in Matthew 15:19, "Out of the heart proceed evil thoughts, murders, adulteries, fornications, thefts, false witness, blasphemies." Today we have an epidemic of people with heart problems, and it has nothing to do with high cholesterol.

In the Bible, when Nicodemus came to see Jesus for advice, Jesus told him that he needed to be "born again" (John 3:3). If that conversation had taken place in today's computer age, Jesus might have told him, "Nicodemus, your heart needs to be reprogrammed; you need a new operating system."

If you want to snakeproof your home, this is also where you need to start. You have to have Christ in your heart, and you need to help your children come to a saving knowledge of Jesus, because without Jesus, there will be no heart change. And without a heart change, you're going down in today's society, so far as sin is concerned, even if you take pornography out of the picture altogether.

2. Let the Air Out of Satan's Lies

Remember the Meat-Bone Principle? It takes something better to give up something bad. You're going to have to spend some time sitting down with your children helping them to understand the values of life.

At some time in your life you probably have been in a swimming pool where there were inflatable balls and toys. And if you've had a beach ball in the swimming pool, sooner or later, you've tried to hold it under the water. You may succeed if you concentrate on what you're doing. If you have two beach balls, it is a lot harder, but you still may be able to do it. With three, it's next to impossible.

Even if you manage to hold a beach ball under the water, you will not be able to do it very long. The moment you get distracted and let go, even for a split second, what happens? Up it comes!

That's the way it is with bad thoughts based on Satan's lies. You say, "I'm not going to think that way; I'm not going to dwell on that thought," and you just kind of push it down into the subconscious. You hold it down and try to concentrate on something else, and up it comes.

All of us have fought that kind of mental battle, have we not? We just keep pushing the beach ball down, but what if we are trying to keep two or three under? You let go of this one to fight that one, and you've got some real problems.

Let me tell you the way to keep those balls under the water. Let the air out of them! What you need to do mentally is let the air out of Satan's lies. Satan is a liar, and one of his greatest lies in our age is pornography. Porn is a lie about sexuality, family, pleasure, and God.

The lie is that porn will give joy; it is something that will give pleasure and fulfillment. Whatever it is, if people didn't think there was some payoff in it, they wouldn't do it. Right?

They do it because they think, *I'm going to get some fun. I'm going to get some pleasure. I'm going to get some fulfillment. I'm going to express myself.* But anything they believe that causes them to do that is based on a lie.

Satan wants to kill—not just the body. He wants to bring death to beauty, happiness, joy, families, purity, and holiness. He just wants to kill. Sin thrills, and then it kills. It fascinates; then it assassinates. Satan is a murderer. His motive is murder. His method is the lie.

"You are of your father the devil, and the desires of your father you want to do. He was a murderer from the beginning, and does not stand in the truth, because there is no truth in him. When he speaks a lie, he speaks from his own resources, for he is a liar and the father of it" (John 8:44).

I once heard a story about a man who was walking down the road with a basket on his arm. In that basket he had some beans, and he was dropping them on the ground. There were some pigs coming along, gobbling them up.

Somebody asked, "What are you doing? Why do you feed your pigs that way?"

"Oh," he replied, "I'm not feeding them. This is the way I get them to the slaughterhouse."

Pornography is much that way. It's Satan's basket of beans with which he wants to destroy.

Let's let the air out of Satan's lies about porn:

THE FUN LIE

Satan calls it harmless fun. But read what the Supreme Court has stated in the case of *Paris Theatre v. Slaton*: "The sum of experience, including that of the past two decades, affords an ample basis for legislatures to conclude that a sensitive, key relationship of human existence, central to family life, community welfare and the development of human personality, can be debased and distorted by crass commercial exploitation of sex."

The warm flames of lust turn to destructive fires of passion and leave a burned-out life.

THE PRIVATE MORALITY LIE

Satan says that porn is harmless. The truth is that it is a mental and moral virus that corrupts everywhere it goes. Porn outlets breed and attract violent crime.[1]

THE DEFINITION LIE

Satan says you can't define obscenity. For that matter, one cannot define in legal terms love, hate, or other emotional expressions. An honest person knows porn when faced with it.

THE PERSONAL FREEDOM LIE

Satan fails to state that porn in the marketplace pollutes the environment as much as chemical pollutants might do. A person is free to choose, but not free to choose the consequences of his choice. It is not true freedom, but bondage of the soul. "For he who sows to his flesh will of the flesh reap corruption, but he who sows to the Spirit will of the Spirit reap everlasting life" (Gal. 6:8).

3. Cover Your Family with Prayer

Pray for your children. Pray for them every day. Let God cover you and protect your home and scatter the enemy when you pray. What did Jesus teach us? Jesus taught us to pray every day, "And lead us not into temptation, but deliver us from evil" (Matt. 6:13 KJV). Satan wants to sabotage your home, and he's already put the dynamite in place, the fuse is laid, and the match is struck.

We sally forth sometimes in the morning and we think, *Well, everything's going fine, I'm not going to have any trouble.* But then we turn the corner, and we meet some unusual temptation.

Here's what sin often is. Sin is a combination of three things:

- an *unexpected* temptation,
- an *undetected* weakness, and
- an *unprotected* life.

An unexpected temptation. Here's a man, perhaps, trying to find something in a search engine on his computer, and up pops pornography. There it is in living color. An unexpected exposure.

An undetected weakness. He did not realize what might be in his heart. The old flesh principle is lurking in the human heart waiting for a door to be opened so it can spring out.

An unprotected life. He didn't pray in the morning, "Lord, lead me not into temptation, but deliver me from evil." He did not put on the whole armor of God, and Satan's dart found the vulnerable spot. Even if your children do not pray for protection, you should still cover them with your protecting prayer.

4. Be a Positive Example

Don't let your children get their sexual identity from the twisted and distorted values of the media and entertainment moguls.

The message of Hollywood and the porn industry is that the idea of a monogamous marriage where a man and woman really love each other is a perversion. They cannot conceive that such is really possible in our society. A happy and wholesome Hollywood family is as rare as a snowstorm in July.

Children need to see the joy and passion of a faithful marriage modeled before them. Let them hear the husband praise his wife for her charm and beauty. She doesn't have to look like a fashion model to win his admiration.

Let the wife brag on Daddy. "He is so strong." "He can fix it." "He's my handsome prince."

Your kids should not get their ideas about romantic love from those who talk the most about it and know the least about it—the media crowd.

Let them see their parents model real love. You don't have to put your intimate life on display, but it wouldn't hurt to let them walk in and catch the two of you locked in an embrace.

Sadly, many kids have grown up where wholesome sexuality is seldom seen or demonstrated. Other homes are led by single parents who cannot model that love. In the case of the single parent, the challenge is to find friends and groups that present positive role models and let your kids see healthy, loving homes.

5. Build Some Guardrails to Keep from Falling

Here is a key verse with rich insight: "When you build a new house, then you shall make a parapet for your roof, that you may not bring bloodguiltiness on your house if anyone falls from it" (Deut. 22:8). A parapet is a safety barrier, a wall several feet high. In the Middle East today, you can still see these parapet walls on the rooftops of houses, the same as in Bible times.

Back then, people lived a lot on the rooftop. It was a patio—a place where they would come up in the evening and sit. Sometimes they would have their meals up there. They would dry their clothes up there.

God said, "When you build a new house, put a wall around the roof." Why? To keep somebody from falling off. If you don't put a wall there and they fall, then their blood is on your hands.

Let's apply that to protecting our kids from falling. Ultimately, there is absolutely nothing you can do to keep your kids from watching pornography, because God gave them a will. But I'll tell you one thing I don't want to be guilty of. I don't want to build a home that is dangerous for my children. If they foolishly climbed over the wall and jumped off, that would break my heart. But I don't want to have the kind of home where they fall accidentally because I have failed to remove the temptations from that home. Do you understand what I am saying? You need at least to build the wall. What are some guardrails parents can build?

GUARD THE USE OF THE COMPUTER

If you can't handle it, take an ax to it. Do not have any on-line service without a good filter.

Put the computer in a public area in your home. Do not let your teen have a computer alone in his or her bedroom. Just don't do it. They'll scream. Let them scream. Put it in the den. Put it in the family room. Place it with the screen in view.

Spend some time on the Internet with your child. See what he or she is watching. If you need to, learn something about it yourself (see chapter 8, "Education: Are You Cyberliterate?"). Teach your children never to open up an unsolicited e-mail from someone they do not know.

If your child has a password for his computer, make him give it to you. You may never have to use it. But let him give it to you. And if he doesn't like it, tough! I'm telling you, your children are your responsibility. Say to them, "You want that computer? If so, you're not going to have any secrets from me. What is there that you don't want me to know about? I'm not going to be snooping. But God wants me to protect you. Child, I would lay down my life for you."

Limit the time your children spend on the computer. If they find anything objectionable, let them feel free to come and talk to you about it. Don't put them down for finding it. Commend them for sharing it with you.

Tell them never to fill out any kind of a questionnaire without your knowledge and your permission. And be careful before you give it.

Learn to Tame the Television

Television, both cable and network, is sinking deeper and deeper into the slime pit. What formerly amazed us now just amuses us. It is said that if you drop a frog into hot water he will jump out. But if you place him in cold water and gradually turn up the heat, you can boil him to death without him realizing it. This is an illustration of the entertainment industry and the American family that is being killed by degrees. Consider this alarming article from the *National Liberty Journal*:

> In September, the Parents Television Council released
> a study documenting the demise of the "family hour,"
> the 8:00 P.M. to 9:00 P.M. time slot television networks
> once reserved for family-friendly programming.
>
> In present-day programming, that time period, once
> reserved for family comedies and dramas, is now riddled
> with "foul language" and "sexual activity," the study
> found. The group disparaged such programming during
> the hour because it is the time when most families are
> likely to be in the television audience.

In the PTC's report, titled, "The Family Hour:
Worse Than Ever and Headed for New Lows," the group
discovered the average of objectionable content has risen
a startling 75% during the past year and a half.
Additionally, during that same time, references to sex acts
have increased 77%. Furthermore, 68% of all shows in
the "family hour" contain sexual material. The PTC
found that 41% of last season's family-hour broadcasts
were ultimately "unsuitable for children."

In the past, parents could be fairly confident that
television programming would not delve into adult
themes during the time slot. With the rise in popularity
of cable programming, video rentals, pay-per-view
movies and the Internet, television programmers feel they
must compete with these outlets by presenting more violent and sexual shows. Despite the popularity of shows
such as *7th Heaven* and *Touched by an Angel*, the expedition
into sexuality has escalated. "They're appealing to the
lowest common denominator," said PTC Executive
Director Mark Honig. "It's much easier to write a cheap
joke with sexual innuendo than address weighty family
issues."

Often the TV is another babysitter. Suppose you said to your
five-year-old one evening, "I'm busy, so you go look in the neighbor's
bedroom window and entertain yourself." The neighbors in this case
are an unmarried couple living in sin. Does it become more acceptable when it is on a TV screen?

Or would you let a dirty minded adult who wants to corrupt your kids be a babysitter? In effect, that is what you do when you let the kids surf the channels. Mom and Dad, wise up!

Don't think that your kids are not affected by what they watch. Why do major advertisers spend millions of dollars each year buying thirty-second commercials if what we see does not affect our behavior? They know that buying habits can be affected in seconds. What then could be the effect of a two-hour, sex-saturated movie?

Listen to Randy Alcorn:

Suppose I said, "There's a great-looking girl down the street. Let's go look through her window and watch her undress, then pose for us naked, from the waist up. Then this girl and her boyfriend will get in a car and have sex—let's listen and watch the windows steam up!"

You'd be shocked. You'd think, "What a pervert!"

But suppose instead I said, "Hey, come on over. Let's watch *Titanic*.

Christians recommend this movie, church youth groups view it together, and many have shown it in their homes. Yet the movie contains precisely the scenes I described.

How does something shocking and shameful somehow become acceptable because we watch it through a television instead of a window?

In terms of the lasting effects on our minds and morals, what's the difference? Yet many think, *Titanic*? Wonderful! It wasn't even rated R!

Every day Christians across the country, including many church leaders, watch people undress through the window of television. We peek on people committing fornication and adultery, which our God calls an abomination. We've become voyeurs, Peeping Toms, entertained by sin.

Let me make some suggestions.

1. You need to cancel some of the movie channel subscriptions that are coming into your home—what I call "Hell's Box Office." All of the major movie channels have viewing fare that is objectionable, but HBO, Cinemax, and Showtime are the absolute worst. My recommendation is that you never subscribe to these under any circumstances, even if they come "free" in a premium channel package. Your kids don't need to watch most of what is on these channels, and neither do you. Just cancel them. You say, "But the movies . . ." Cancel it! Get it out! Find a cable or satellite package that you can live with. And even there you're going to have to monitor.

2. Remove or block out all channels that are known for racy material. Start with MTV and go from there. Most televisions now come with the capability to program out certain channels. If you have cable or satellite TV, the capability to order pay-per-view movies is usually built right in. Contact your cable or satellite company or read your instruction manual to make sure that this capability is limited and restricted on all of the television sets in your house. Check your cable or satellite bill to see if anyone is ordering unauthorized pay-per-view events.

3. Consider installing some type of device that filters or restricts access to objectionable content. These options are discussed in further detail in chapter 9, "Protection."

4. Kids don't need a TV set in their bedroom. Let them go to the bedroom to sleep, not to watch who knows what.

5. Set a limit on the time spent watching TV. For example: "You have two hours to watch TV today, so spend it wisely." The TV set is not to be on continually.

6. Let all TV viewing be first cleared by parents. A little common sense can help here. There are good reviews available. Here are three Web sites that review TV shows from a Christian perspective:

- www.christiananswers.net/spotlight/tv/home.html
- www.gospelcom.net/preview
- www.parentstv.org

7. Find creative substitutes for TV. Bring back family games and adventures. Get out of the house together. Let the kids learn to read great books. Let them have friends over often.

GET RID OF QUESTIONABLE CDs, VIDEOS, AND MAGAZINES

You need to get the trash out of the house. Start by playing a game with your kids: What if Jesus were coming to your house to spend the week? He would sleep in one of your bedrooms. He would be able to browse through all of the videos, CDs, and magazines that are lying around. Let's clean up the house before company comes. Talk about CDs with objectionable lyrics, novels or magazines that condone premarital sex (*Cosmo, Glamour*, etc.), and certain MTV-type shows that would be made "off-limits." These are the areas where we are helping our kids by "putting up a guard rail to keep them from falling." Helpful points:

1. Establish a family agreement about which TV shows are off-limits. Have the kids participate to establish the standards.

2. Have a standards policy for lyrics on recordings.

3. Have a list of magazines that are inappropriate.

4. The WWJD standard: Would I listen to or watch this if Jesus were sitting here in the room?

Screen Movies Carefully

Hollywood is systematically seducing our kids. Money-motivated movie moguls have little concern for your kids' welfare. Moms and dads who don't monitor what types of movies their kids see—either on TV or at the theater—may be in for an unpleasant surprise.

A recent study conducted by researchers at Dartmouth College focused on finding out if kids whose parents let them watch R-rated movies were affected by the behavior of characters in those movies—characters who typically drink and smoke more than those in other films. The results of the study, which involved more than four thousand fifth-graders through eighth-graders, were revealing:

"Among those who had no restrictions on R-rated films, they were more likely to have tried both tobacco and alcohol," said Jennifer Tickle, who worked on the study. Among kids who regularly watched R-rated films, nearly 50% had tried alcohol and more than 33% had tried smoking. However, of those kids whose parents banned such movies, only 4% had tried alcohol and 2% smoking. Indeed, the study found that parents restricting their kids' movie-viewing had greater impact than any other parenting characteristic they measured.

Although other behaviors such as violence, cursing and habitual lying were not measured in the study, some pro-family leaders believe such movie content could have an equally pronounced impact on kids.

"It just makes sense that a kid who is sympathetic to the cussing, lying, 'blow-'em-away' hero of their favorite

movie will be influenced by that character's actions," said
AFA president Don Wildmon.[2]

Once you make the decision to enforce a tougher movie
policy, brace yourself, because this is where you will have a real
battle. Your kids will go to school and everybody else will be
asking, "Have you seen so and so?" And your child will say, "No,
I haven't seen that." And he will feel like an outsider.

I had to fight this battle with my kids. "But Dad, everybody
. . . Dad, Mike's parents let him . . . Dad, John is allowed to see
that." Just love them. But teach them that they are not different;
they are distinctive. Teach them how to stand alone.

Here is what Joe McNamara, writing in *USA Today*, has to say
about combating Hollywood's propensity for sex and violence in
the movies:

> There is plenty viewers can do to protest this trend.
> Just three of the 25 best-selling videos of all times have
> an "R" rating. Go buy the other 22 and show them
> repeatedly. Watch many of the classics made before the
> first "R" rating in 1968, because 60% of the films made
> after that were "R" or worse. Look for the Dove
> Foundation's blue-and-white label on videos the Grand
> Rapids, Mich., organization rates as "family friendly," or
> sponsor a low-cost, multi-film festival they can help you
> set up.
>
> Open that most radical of books, the Bible, and talk
> about the revelations of Revelation. Get some of the
> best of PBS, like "Shadowlands" and Ken Burns, and
> ignore most of the ideology-laden glop they throw at
> you. Explain to your kids that masterpieces teach you

something new about yourself every time you see them, and then watch them again. Revisit older musicals and newer versions (after viewing the latter yourself first). Watch historical footage, especially of combat, with older kids, and explain that all this was done in the name of freedom. Convert your church social hall or service club to a mini-theater and offer a weekly film festival of your own. Keep cheesy film-gossip magazines out of your house and out of your life.

Work to establish a money-back guarantee at motion picture theaters. Most honest merchants have one. If you leave the movie within the first 20 minutes, you should have a right to get your money back because you were dissatisfied with what your ticket bought you.

The real trick is how to do this without seeming to be overbearing and out of touch with your children and their friends. There are usually no fanfares or overtures for unsung heroes. The best music comes later.

When it comes to screening movies for your kids, you don't have to act in a vacuum. Here is a partial list of Web sites that review movies for families based on content and acceptability:

- Ted Baehr's Movie Guide www.movieguide.org
- FamilyStyle Film Guide www.familystyle.com
- Family Movie Reviews Online
  www.familymoviereviews.com
- Preview Family Movie & TV Review
  www.previewonline.org (subscription required)
- Grading the Movies www.gradingthemovies.com

Listing of these Web sites is for your information. I am in no way endorsing everything you will read or see. These sites list the objectionable content of each movie, so they may be unsuitable for your children to use alone. Remember, you are the final filter.

A final word of caution: Don't assume that just because a particular movie is aimed at kids that it is acceptable. As an example, a check of *Scooby-Doo 2: Monsters Unleashed* (Warner Brothers, 2004) on the familystyle.com Web site reveals why it is rated PG: Moderate profanity (including deity), scantily clad females, cleavage, brief conversation about sex, intense and graphic violence, and accepted alcohol and tobacco use.

6. Don't Be "Home Alone"

Give your home a positive atmosphere—from encouraging Scripture mottoes on the wall to the right kind of music on the stereo. Plan wholesome entertainment. Spend some time choosing the right television programs, the right videotapes and DVDs, the right games.

Make your home the best place in the neighborhood to be. Make it the kind of place that your children's friends want to come to. Let your home ring with laughter. Let it be permeated with love.

Keep plenty of food in the refrigerator. Encourage the kids to raid it. Let them soil your rugs. Let them break down your couch because too many kids sat on it. So what! Let your home be a good place, a fun place, a happy place.

7. Help Your Children Choose Friends Carefully

Here's another benefit of making your home the place where all the kids want to hang out: Your kids will bring his friends there, and you can look them over. A little discernment will help you help your kids choose quality friends. Remember that Scripture teaches that "the companion of fools will be destroyed" (Prov. 13:20).

HAVE AN AGREED-ON POLICY FOR STAYING WITH FRIENDS AND SLEEPOVERS

Even if you provide hands-on monitoring of what your children and their friends watch in your home, you have to be careful when you let your children stay with others overnight. When surveyed about their first exposure to pornographic magazines, 77 percent said this happened at a friend's house. Don't assume that because the parents of your child's friends are church members or "good Christians" that their standards will be the same as yours.

At the risk of sounding overbearing or narrow, I suggest before your child spends the night (or the afternoon, for that matter) with a friend that you call the parents. Tell them your family's standards for TV and video fare. For example, you might say, "Brad is not allowed to watch any R-rated or PG-13 rated videos. He is only allowed to watch PG-rated movies with his parent's prior approval."

Many families own videos or DVDs that are not suitable for children to watch. Be sure to ask about how the watching of movies is supervised, and make sure that the children will not be left by themselves with unrestricted access to any movie in the family video library.

Encourage your children to take some initiative. At some point in time, your child will probably be somewhere where a movie is going to be shown. If it is your family policy, teach them to say, "I can't watch that until I first call home, because my parents won't let me watch any video without first calling them."

Don't assume because the parents rent the move and watch it with the children that it is okay. Many parents have no common sense or spiritual sensibility when it comes to what they let their children watch, let alone what they watch themselves.

Return to Sender

In conclusion, let me say if "the snake's in the mail" and it's addressed to your house, send it back unopened and marked— DELIVERY REFUSED!

Endnotes

1. Numerous institutional studies have confirmed a direct link between the use of pornography and violent crime. Here is a partial list of some significant case studies:

Goldstein, Kant and Harman (1973)
Malamuth (1978)
Malamuth and Check (1980)
Donnerstein and Berkowitz (1981)
Silbert and Pines (1981)
Zillmann and Bryant (1982)
Baron and Straus (1984)
Donnerstein and Linz (1985)
Zillmann and Bryant (1986 and 1988)
Violato, Paolicci, and Genius (2002)

A sample finding from one of these studies: Rapists are fifteen times as likely as non-offenders to have had exposure to hard-core pornography during childhood or between six and ten years of age *(Goldstein, Kant and Harman, 1973)*.

2. *Family News in Focus,* March 6, 2002.

∽ 7 ∽

Making a Family Covenant:

Ganging Up on the Devil

The home is under attack, and it is time we circled the wagons.
We need to bring the family together, explain the situation,
and make plans to protect the things that mean the most to us. In

these days parents and kids need to be on
the same team. Yet all that we can do
together is not enough without the protection of our heavenly Father. Psalm
127 makes this clear: "Unless the Lord
builds the house, they labor in vain who

∽

*Tolerance today is
the great enemy of
Christian purity.*

∽

build it; unless the Lord guards the city, the watchman stays awake in vain" (Ps. 127:1).

We need to remember that God himself is the builder and the protector of the home. We must continually look to him, pray to him, and believe in him. This does not mean that there is nothing for us to do. The Bible speaks of a family warfare. "Lo, children are an heritage of the LORD: and the fruit of the womb is his reward. As arrows are in the hand of a mighty man; so are children of the youth. Happy is the man that hath his quiver full of them: they shall not be ashamed, but they shall speak with the enemies in the gate" (Ps. 127:3–5 KJV). These verses teach us that there is an enemy in the gate. Fathers are like warriors and the children are like arrows.

It's All-out War!

The warrior must be strong *("a mighty man")*. If there was ever a time for fathers to be mighty men of God, this is the time. God give us men of strength. I am not talking about financial, physical, or intellectual strength. These are well and good, but the great need is mighty men (and women) of faith—warriors who know how to bend the bow of prayer. Parents who themselves have hearts that are pure and strong for the battle.

The arrow must be straight *("arrows are in the hand")*. The Scripture speaks of children as arrows in the hand of a strong warrior. Children are not born arrows. They are born sticks. They need to be made into arrows. They need to be straightened, polished, and pointed. A man cannot shoot with crooked arrows. There are many today who would like to warp the lives of our children.

They do this under the banner of the false god whose name is Tolerance. Tolerance today is the great enemy of Christian purity. Tolerance puts a bend in the arrow that should not be there and gives it a blunt end. Tolerance in some matters is a virtue, but the state religion today seems to be the religion of tolerance. No longer is it sufficient to "love your neighbor." Now our kids are taught, "Not only must you love your neighbor but you must tolerate all of his or her behavior." "If you don't agree with that behavior, you must repent because you are not to judge." "Embrace all people and their behavior, or else you are the one who is wrong."

Only a fool would deny that tolerance can be a virtue. There are issues on which we should be open-minded, circumstances that require forbearance, and some areas in which we need to live and let live; but tolerance that calls for the abandonment of conviction is of hell!

Tolerance is sometimes incompatible with basic truth. It is dangerous to play make believe. G. K. Chesterton said it wisely: "Tolerance is the virtue for those who do not believe much."

The aim must be sure *("they shall speak with the enemies in the gate").* Our children need not be only on the defensive, but militantly on the offensive. Arrows are made to be shot at the enemy. There is an enemy, and in this war we cannot be neutral. It is time that we got serious about the values that we hold deeply and those who would destroy them.

United We Stand

One way to do that would be to make a *family covenant.* The entire family needs to come together for the battle, and they need to covenant with one another to support one another in the fight.

Why make a family covenant? You know one of the most dia-
bolical lies of the devil is the concept of "adult entertainment." We
see this advertised all the time: "adult entertainment." It is not
adult. It is infantile, and it is wicked. Do you know what the concept of adult entertainment says to a child? "Now look, you can't
watch this because you're not old enough. It's all right for Dad; it's
all right for Mom; it's just not all right for you. But one of these
days, you'll be old enough to enjoy what we enjoy." You talk about
phony baloney; friend, that is phony baloney. A covenant must be
for every member of the family.

How do you make a family covenant? You as a father get the
family together and you say, "Children, we're going to make some
promises to one another." Let's suppose your little girl's name is
Susan. "Susan, Daddy believes that pornography is wrong. He
wants you to be able to love. He wants you to be able to have
fellowship with God. He wants you to have a happy family. Daddy
wants our family to be happy.

"So I want to make covenant with you, Susan. I want to
promise you in your mother's presence and promise your mother
that I will never watch any entertainment in your absence that
I would not watch in your presence. I promise you before God.
And Susan, we want you to make a covenant with us. We want
you to make a promise to us before God that you will never watch
any entertainment in our absence that you would not watch in
our presence."

Then write that covenant out and sign it before God on your
knees.

A Covenant of Love

We the undersigned solemnly and joyfully make
this covenant of love.
We agree that among our highest values are our fellowship with
God, the ability to love and be loved, and the sanctity of the
Christian family.
We further agree that ungodly and impure (pornographic)
involvement and entertainment are
harmful and hurtful to the blessings God wants for us.
We also solemnly agree that we need to prayerfully encourage one
another in the building and maintaining of lives of mental and
moral purity that lead to godly fellowship,
loving relationships, and family values.
Therefore, with deep dependence upon God and in covenant
with one another we promise:

- To seek God with a pure heart and walk daily in fellowship with him.
- To refrain from allowing evil and sensual materials into
  our hearts and minds through films, videos, books, magazines, CDs, or other avenues.
- Not to watch any form of entertainment while apart from
  the others that we could not mutually enjoy together. This
  will be true for the whole family—adults and children.
- To be open, vulnerable, and accountable to one another.
  We can freely be challenged, encouraged, and admonished
  by one another.

We make this covenant with humility and love and look to
Almighty God to help us to keep it.
God being our helper we will.
The undersigned:

How to Stay on Track

After the covenant is signed, here are some practical helps to keep you on track:

HAVE A SYMBOL OR TOKEN OF YOUR COVENANT

Would you be willing to put a padlock on your heart, on your emotions, your devotion? Then would you take the key and give it to your wife, your husband, or your children? This may be symbolized with a literal key, maybe gold-plated, a key that your daughter could wear around her neck and your son and you could keep on a key chain. Some other symbol would work also.

When you exchange these symbols, you might say to your daughter, for example, "Darling, keep this. Carry it with you. I'll put my name on it and you give me one like it with your name on it. It reminds us that we are in covenant together before God and that ours is a holy covenant with a mighty God."

Every businessman with that kind of a key on his key chain ought to remember the holy vows he has made to his wife and the covenant he has signed with his children.

DON'T FORGET SCRIPTURE MEMORY

I remind you of the chapter on "Staying Clean in a Dirty World." A major emphasis that we put in that chapter was on Scripture memory. In order to help you do this, we have included in the back of this book one hundred Bible memory verses (appendix I, page 162).

∽

Carry a picture of your family with you on every business trip. When you unpack, put it on top of the television set.

∽

These verses have been chosen specifically to help you and your family replace corrosive thoughts with edifying truth.

Copy these out and distribute them to members of the family. This will be a great source of strength if the family memorizes Scripture together.

MINIMIZE TEMPTATION WHEN DADS TRAVEL

Ask to have all sexually explicit channels blocked when you check into the hotel. Don't feel foolish or sheepish about doing this. To the contrary, it may open the door to a great witnessing opportunity. At least, it will be your way of saying that you don't want that filth in a room that you have rented.

Once inside don't channel surf. Decide what you want to watch and go directly to that channel. If you come up with something offensive, have enough courage, fortitude, and honesty to move away from it quickly.

Carry a picture of your family with you on every business trip. When you unpack, put it on top of the television set. Begin and end your business day with the Bible and prayer. Keep your Bible out in the room. Every night call home and express your love to your wife and children and pray with them.

KIDS AT SCHOOL SHOULD TAKE THE INITIATIVE IN THEIR FAITH

Be a bold Christian so those who want to spread their filthy virus will not feel welcomed to do so. Don't be obnoxious or "holier-than-thou," but stand up for your faith. Let people know where you stand. The best defense is a good offense. I don't mean be offensive, but I mean be strong and militant for Jesus. You might carry your Bible to school and certainly bring your memory verses with you.

SHARE YOUR VICTORIES AND FAILURES WITH OTHER MEMBERS IN THE FAMILY

Be open, honest, and vulnerable. Don't have secrets in this area. If you fail, confess it to God and other family members. Ask them to pray for you. This will open their hearts to share their failures as well.

OUTSIDE OF YOUR FAMILY HAVE SOMEONE WITH WHOM YOU ARE ACCOUNTABLE

Meet with this person on a regular basis. Here are some suggested questions:

1. What about your relationship with God? Have you been spending regular time in the Word and in prayer?

2. How is your relationship with your mate? If a young person, the question may be: How is your relationship with your parents?

3. What temptations are you facing and how are you dealing with them? How has your thought life been this week? Have you watched any obscene, impure material?

4. In your answers to any of these questions, have you told me the absolute truth?

5. How can I pray for you and help you?

May God help moms and dads to take the lead. May God help kids to get on the team. The battle is real, and the enemy is strong, but victory is possible!

PART II

A Battle Plan

∽ 8 ∽

Education:
Are You Cyberliterate?

So far we've discussed some valuable spiritual and practical principles to help you guard your heart and protect your home. In chapter 2 we learned how you can be a hero to your kids. In chapter 4, we thought about how to help kids say no to pornography by learning to discern trash from treasure. In chapter 5, we studied how to have a pure thought life—how to stay clean in a dirty world. In chapter 6, we learned how to let the air out of Satan's lies, and about how God holds us responsible to build guardrails to protect our family. In chapter 7, we thought about waging spiritual warfare against the enemy by making a family covenant.

In the remaining chapters of this book, I'd like to give you a battle action plan. With this plan, I want you to take all of the valuable lessons we've learned so far and put them into practice. This plan is simple, straightforward, and extremely practical, but it will take determination, patience, and perseverance on your part. Remember, when it comes to protecting your home in an X-rated world, there are no shortcuts, quick fixes, or easy answers.

This battle action plan has four steps that should be followed in order. Each step can be summarized in a single word. The four steps are:

- Education
- Protection
- Involvement
- Awareness

The first two steps, *education* and *protection*, are steps that you, as a parent, can take by yourself. The last two steps, *involvement* and *awareness*, will involve interaction with your family.

This chapter covers the first step in our four-step battle action plan—education. In the following chapter dealing with protection, we will discuss practical ways you can filter the filth that enters your home electronically. But before we begin to talk about filters, you may need to do some remedial computer education. Let's start with a pop quiz.

Quick, what do the following have in common: RAM, ROM, CPU, ICQ, USB, ISP, SSL, GUI and DSL? Answer: They are a few of the hundreds of acronyms and abbreviations that populate the computer world. If you find yourself unable to enter into the conversation when terms like these are being bandied about, don't fret. It's simply time for you to take a crash course on basic computing or buy a book like *Computers for Dummies,* and bone up on the "geek-speak."

(If you want to know what the above list of acronyms means, take a deep breath and repeat after me: Random Access Memory, Read Only Memory, Central Processing Unit, I Seek You, Universal Serial Bus, Internet Service Provider, Secure Socket Layers, Graphical User Interface, and Digital Subscriber Line.)

The Great Cyber-Divide

One of the fascinating aspects of today's information society is that, in many cases, the kids—from preschooler to teenager—know a lot more about computers than the parents do.

If you fall into this category, you are at a real disadvantage when it comes to putting filters in place, or even monitoring your children's computer activity. My admonition to you is this: Don't have it in your home if you don't know how to use it.

I'm Online—Now What?

At this point in the book, I am going to assume that you have a computer in your home and have some type of online service (AOL, MSN, Earthlink, local ISP, etc.). I'm also going to assume that you already have a basic knowledge of computing and the Internet. Although the terms "being online" and "being on the Internet (or Web)" are sometimes used interchangeably, the World Wide Web is just one aspect of being online. As a parent, there are six basic components of online computing that you need to be aware of. I will describe them first and then list some cautions and guidelines for each:

The World Wide Web

When most people refer to the Internet, they are speaking of the World Wide Web, commonly referred to as simply "the Web." Although the World Wide Web is technically a component of the Internet, for almost all purposes, the terms can be used interchangeably. You need a Web browser to browse, or surf, the Net.

E-mail

You send and receive e-mail using either a dedicated e-mail program (called an e-mail client), or Web-based e-mail (which simply means that you go to a Web page to send and receive your e-mail).

Instant Messaging

With the proper software installed on your computer, instant messaging, or IM for short, allows you to "talk" in real time to friends who are online. The most popular instant messaging software is by AOL and is called AIM (AOL Instant Messaging). Other popular IM programs include MSN Messenger, Yahoo Messenger, and ICQ. Once you log on to an IM program, it allows you to instantly send and receive text messages with any of your friends who are also logged in to the instant messaging program.

News Groups and Bulletin Boards

In addition to the World Wide Web, news groups comprise a vast area of the Internet. You can subscribe to or join any number of news groups, ranging from hobbies such as cooking, gardening, and classic cars to the most vile perversions and practices imaginable. News groups are accessed by using a news reader. A news reader can be a standalone software application, or is often included in e-mail programs such as Microsoft Outlook. Some news readers are also Web-based, meaning they can be accessed from a news group Web site.

Bulletin boards are similar to news groups. Most bulletin boards are moderated (which means the content is monitored to prevent obscenity and flamers), whereas most news groups are not. In moderated groups, any message sent to the group is first routed to the moderator. The moderator determines if the content is appropriate for the discussion group and then forwards it to everyone in the discussion group.

The largest news group is called Usenet. Usenet has thousands of different news groups, many of which are pornographic in nature.

CLUBS AND GROUPS

Clubs, also known simply as groups, are online communities where information about a subject of common interest is exchanged. Clubs are similar to news groups, but most have several important differences. Usually, you must register and create a user profile to join a club. Clubs are usually accessed through Web portals such as Yahoo and MSN. Though a lot of clubs are beneficial in nature, many should be avoided at all costs.

CHAT ROOMS (IRC)

Chat rooms are similar to Instant Messaging, in that conversations are conducted in real time. The difference is that most of the people in a chat room don't know each other, as participants are identified only by a screen name. Chat rooms are usually accessed through a Web site, and are usually based on a common topic of interest.

Guidelines for Being Online

All six of these components—the World Wide Web, e-mail, instant messaging, news groups, clubs, and chat rooms—can be lumped together collectively as "being online." However, as a parent, you should approach each of these online components in one of three ways: (1) **the World Wide Web and e-mail,** use with supervision; (2) **instant messaging,** use with extreme caution; and (3) **news groups, clubs, and chat rooms,** just say *no.*

Let me elaborate:

1. THE WEB AND E-MAIL: USE WITH SUPERVISION

The World Wide Web and e-mail should be used by your children with your direct supervision. In addition to installing a filtering system, which I will talk about in the chapter on "Fences, Firewalls, and Filters," you may want to have a list of approved Web sites that your children are only allowed to visit. Teach your children never to open unsolicited e-mail, and never to open attachments without knowing what they are. If you decide to let your child have his individual e-mail address, make sure you have access to the password and account settings.

Beware of Web mail. Unfortunately, even if you scrupulously monitor and control the setting up of e-mail accounts in your e-mail software (such as Outlook Express, Netscape, or AOL), any child left to himself for ten minutes can create a Web-based e-mail account using a free Web mail service such as Juno, Hotmail, or Yahoo. The user goes to a Web page to send and receive e-mail. If he decides to do so, your child can set up several Web-based e-mail addresses that he can access from any computer. Because these e-mail addresses will be password-protected (by a password your child chooses), you will not be able to access these pages to see what your child has been sending or receiving.

What about privacy? This brings up an interesting point: Should you read your child's "personal" e-mail? Let me put it this way. Let's suppose you have a fourteen-year old boy whose friend is sending him dirty magazines in the mail. You confront him, and let him know, in no uncertain terms, that any mail that arrives in the family mailbox is subject to screening.

You then find out that he has opened a post office box in his name at the post office, and is having his friend send the dirty magazines there. When you discover this and confront him again, he replies, "This is my private mail. It comes to me at my private mail box. You have no right to read my private mail. You are violating my right to privacy."

What should you do? I hope you would demand the post office box be closed, and continue to rigorously inspect and monitor all incoming mail. Your *responsibility* as a parent supercedes any supposed *right* to privacy your child may have. The same principle applies to e-mail, as well as to anything else that happens on the computer.

2. INSTANT MESSAGING: USE WITH EXTREME CAUTION

Instant Messaging (IM) is very popular with children of all ages, but especially teens. Are there dangers? You better believe it. Consider these words of warning from the Los Angeles district attorney's office:

The Dangers and Risks Posed by IM
Private Conversations—with Anyone—Are Easy

Used properly, Instant Messaging can be very helpful and practical. Your kids can let you know they got home from school okay without disturbing you at the office. If the phone line is tied up and your child wants to know more about a homework assignment, he or she can IM a classmate to clarify the teacher's instructions. However, if your kids are unaware of the dangers posed by IM, they may not be as cautious about their IM communications as they should be. For all its appeal to young people, IM also poses a number of risks. *An IM-equipped child can communicate anywhere, with anyone, at any time on the IM network—all without a parent's knowledge.*

The Profile Problem

Besides offering real-time contact with strangers or others who may seek to harm your child, Instant Messaging allows for the immediate dissemination of significant personal information. When your child signs up for an IM account, he or she is asked to fill out a personal profile that asks for key identifying information on the account holder. This personal profile is then placed in an Internet directory that can be viewed by all. The directory can be searched by name, date of birth, gender, and interests. Consequently, an unsuspecting child can effectively place himself or herself in a position to receive unsolicited offers of sex, pornography, and other dubious material.

Protecting Your Child in an IM World

Children must know the potential dangers of Instant Messaging to understand why they need to be cautious about how they use it. **Set up rules for Instant Messaging and explain the reason for each rule to your child.** Remember, while you can monitor the family computer's use at home, keep in mind that kids have access to the Internet in a variety of other places—at the homes of friends, at school, at public libraries, etc. **You can protect your child by:**

- Setting limits for the use of IM.
- No IM during homework time—IM can have a negative effect on grades and facilitates cheating.
- No late-night IMs. Fewer children are online late at night.
- Place a time limit on the use of IM.

Reviewing his or her IM profile.

- The profile should contain no personal information. That means no real names, no age, no photos, no telephone numbers, no address—nothing that can identify your child for an Internet predator.
- The profile should not link to a Web site.
- The IM screen name should not be the child's real name.

Monitoring cellular IM links.

To further limit your child's exposure to predators and other inappropriate individuals, you may want to set rules for your child's use of Instant Messages on his or her cellular phone. Your child's friends can make contact by phone, or leave voice mail.

If your child already has an IM link to his or her cell phone and it was obtained without your permission, the Internet Service Provider (ISP) or cellular service provider may be in violation of the Children's Online Privacy Protection Act (COPPA). You can request that the provider stop collecting data on your child. You can also stop the IM service.

Discussing IM safety issues with your child.

- Teach your child to follow good "Netiquette," such as not using or responding to sexually explicit, foul, or hateful language.
- Tell your child not to respond to "flames." A *flame* is a strongly worded, sometimes obscene message sent to a public forum, such as a newsgroup, or to a personal email address. Responding only encourages the other party to become more aggressive or crude.

Knowing your child's IM member number, screen name, and password.

- Make sure your children do not give out their screen names or IM member numbers to people they do not personally know.
- Warn your children not to add individuals to their IM list that they only know from Internet interactions. The ten-year-old "boy" your child converses with in a chat room may really be a 38-year-old man.

Knowing your child's online friends, just as you would know their real-world friends.

Remember, your children should not make online friends without your knowledge and consent. Your children should *never* meet in person with anyone they become acquainted with online without your permission.

Warning your child to be wary of anyone he or she meets in a chat room.

IM programs include adult-oriented chat rooms that should not be accessed by children. Though chat rooms are monitored, keep in mind that no one will ask your child for an ID before he or she enters a chat room. Once a child adds a stranger from a chat room to his or her IM buddy list, their IM conversations are private. In addition, as long as they remain on each other's buddy lists, the stranger will be automatically notified whenever your child goes online.

Chat Room Controls

If your child engages in inappropriate conversations in chat rooms or in private Instant Message conversations, you may consider changing the preferences in your IM program to discontinue chats when certain words come up.[1]

NEWS GROUPS, CLUBS, AND CHAT ROOMS: JUST SAY NO

News Groups. Most news groups are totally uncensored and cannot be recommended for use by children or teens under any circumstances. Any search for information for something like a school research project should be done by using reputable Web portals with safe search filtering in place. (For more information about using "family friendly" search engines/portals, see "Practice Safe Surfing," chapter 9, pages 131–33.) Be especially wary of the "binary" news groups which are set up to share and swap movies, music, and photos. Even if the files to be swapped are not pornographic or lewd in nature, many of them, including almost all music files, are shared illegally.

Some news groups offer free content, but the popular ones charge a monthly subscription fee. A subscription to a news group like Usenet is like paying someone to pipe raw sewage into your home. Sure, there's good information on the news groups. There's good food to be found in many garbage cans, but that doesn't mean you should look for your food there. My advice is don't subscribe to any of these and make sure no one in your family does.

Clubs and Chat Rooms. Clubs, groups, and chat rooms are a great way to create online communities based on a topic of common interest. Unfortunately, sexual predators often lurk in clubs and chat rooms that have kid- or teen-based topics of interest. These predators pose as kids themselves, and many wait patiently for the right moment to seduce an unwitting child. Since the potential harm far outweighs any benefit, my advice is that all commercial groups, clubs, and chat rooms be off-limits at all times for your children.[2]

After reading this chapter, you may not know everything there is to know about being online, but you now know enough to realize its potential danger, and that you, as a parent, cannot afford to be passive. Now it's time to do something about the problem. On to the next chapter—"Protection: Fences, Firewalls, and Filters."

Endnotes

1. District Attorney's Office, County of Los Angeles, Calif., Protecting Our Kids, http://da.co.la.ca.us/pok.

2. I am talking about any club, group, or chat room hosted by a standard online portal or ISP such as Netscape, MSN, even AOL. As an alternative, you may want to consider some of these Christian chat rooms and "safe" clubs designed for children to have a protected online environment: Wonderzone (www.Wonderzone.org), Focus on the Family's Clubhouse (www.clubhousemagazine.com), Praize Kidz (www.praize.com/kidz), or KidSurf Online (www.kidsurf.net).

≈ 9 ≈

Protection:
Fences, Firewalls, and Filters

Ihope by now you are well on your way to educating yourself about the technology (and the inherent dangers) of cyberspace. Now it is time to address the next step—protection. In chapter 6, one of the strategies I gave you for snakeproofing your home was to build some guardrails to keep from falling. In this chapter, I want to give practical help in dealing with one of the areas of greatest concern—the computer. I'll also touch on some safeguards you should be aware of concerning television, videos, and DVDs.

I've subtitled this chapter "Fences, Firewalls, and Filters." I've chosen these three words because, although similar, each one

symbolizes a different aspect of the concept of protecting your home.

Fences. Fences are what we use to
stake a claim to the boundaries of our
property. When someone puts up a fence,
he is saying, "Everything within this
fence is my private property. I am the
guardian of it. Treat it with respect, and
don't trespass here!" Should we do any
less when it comes to our families?

Firewalls. A firewall is sophisticated
software or hardware that computer programmers put in place to keep hackers
from gaining unlawful entry into their
computer system. Unfortunately, there
are hackers out there who want to gain unlawful entry not only to
your computer, but also to your heart and home.

When it comes to the Internet, there is a lot of poison in the water. The good news is that there are solutions available that will help you filter out the junk.

They are what we call cyberpredators, and they are a very real
threat to your children. I'm going to give you some practical advice
to build your own family firewall to keep these cyberpredators out
of your home.

Filters. Filters are everywhere we look. Open the hood of your
car, and the first thing you see is an air filter. What is its purpose?
To let the air into the engine, but keep the dirt out. If you have a
swimming pool, there is a filter in the system. The purpose? To let
the clean water through, but keep the trash out. You may have a filter on the faucet in your kitchen for your drinking water. Why? To
catch the harmful toxins and chemicals before they come through
the tap.

When it comes to the Internet, there is a lot of poison in the water. The good news is that there are solutions available that will help you filter out the junk.

Although I strongly urge you to take advantage of the Internet filtering solutions that are available, don't let technology provide a sense of false security. Consider this Associated Press story by Randolph E. Schmid:

WASHINGTON—Protecting children from pornography on the Internet is too complicated to rely merely on laws or computer programs that try to block sexually explicit material, a National Research Council committee concluded Thursday.

A combination of steps is needed and a crucial factor is the involvement of parents and teachers in educating children, said the committee.

Former U.S. attorney general Richard Thornburgh, chairman of the panel, added that parents and grandparents have an obligation to educate themselves about the Internet so they can guide and supervise children. There's a place for law enforcement and blocking programs but these can be circumvented, he said.

Members also noted that children need to be taught that not everything they read on the Internet is true and to be wary of strangers they may meet in chat rooms who may turn out to be predators.

Panel member Geoffrey Stone of the University of Chicago said that while Internet screening filters and law enforcement can help protect children, "over-reliance on those methods will lead to a false sense of security."

Any purely technological solution can be circumvented and is an incomplete solution. It is not a replacement for parental education, awareness, and involvement.

Throughout the rest of this chapter, and the remaining chapters as well, I'll mention the names of different software companies, Web sites, technology providers, and such. All of this information was current as of press time, but as you are no doubt aware, computer technology and Internet technology in particular change at a frightening pace. By the time you read this, technologies mentioned may be outdated and some companies mentioned may even be out of business. In this event, rest assured the problem will not have gone away, and it will still be your responsibility as a parent to protect your family. We will try to keep up-to-date information on current filtering technology on our Web site: www.guardyourheart.net.

How to Filter the Filth

Here are four practical safeguards you need to implement to guard your heart and protect your home:

I. PUT A FILTER ON YOUR COMPUTER

First, put a security system in place on your computer. Whether you want to believe it or not, chances are that at some point your child will attempt to access inappropriate sexual material online. Consider these real-life examples, as reported by the *Wall Street Journal*:

> Daniel Rosen was brought down by an electronic version of a trail of bread crumbs. While the 13-year-old from West Chester, PA has his own computer and access

to America Online, his parents use AOL's parental controls, which permit Daniel to go only to those Web sites deemed appropriate for young teens. But that wasn't enough to keep Daniel from wandering around the Web. While his parents weren't looking, Daniel broke into his father's AOL account and visited some X-rated Web sites. "He cracked my password," says the boy's dad, Mike Rosen, who is chief executive of an Internet software company in King of Prussia, PA. "He just tried everything he could think of." Daniel says it wasn't all that hard; the password had been saved on the computer.

Mr. Rosen might never have known about the security breach, but his son left electronic fingerprints. Mr. Rosen started getting unsolicited email messages from pornographic Web sites. Curious, he looked at the browser cache on his computer—the record of sites visited—and found addresses with risqué names. Mr. Rosen then checked his cookie file. The porn sites had sent a number of cookies—little computer programs that recognize a returning visitor and track his movements—onto Mr. Rosen's hard drive. Daniel was in big trouble.

"I got busted," Daniel says sheepishly. "I think my dad can see wherever I go."

Many parents can do exactly that. Norm Zurawski, a locksmith in Schofield, Wis., and the father of three children, uses a computer program called Spector to track everything his kids do on the computer. The program takes frequent electronic "snapshots" of the computer screen and lets Mr. Zurawski replay the action later. The kids don't know how he sees what they are doing.

Mr. Zurawski's elder son, 17-year-od Nate, has felt the effect, however. When Nate was caught visiting some pornographic Web sites, his father forbade him to go online for a week. But after Mr. Zurawski unplugged the family's high-speed DSL Internet connection and went to sleep, Nate plugged his computer into a dial-up phone line and got on the Internet using a friend's AOL screen name. "I knew what was going on because I got these AOL screen shots," Mr. Zurawski says.[1]

Perhaps you don't have teenage boys like Daniel or Nate, but a sweet, innocent six- or seven-year-old girl. Do you still need to install a filter on your computer? Absolutely! Do it for your teens. Do it for your preteens. Do it for your spouse. Do it for yourself.

Choose a filter type. There are two basic types of Internet filtering solutions: client-side filtering and server-side filtering. In plain English, the server is your Internet service provider, or online service, and the client is you or your computer. Client-side filtering is software that you install on your computer. Server-side filtering is done by your Internet service provider (or a third-party filtering company) to filter content before it gets to your computer. There are advantages and disadvantages to each.

Client-side filtering. A client-side filter is a software program or package that you install on your computer. Some popular programs include Net Nanny, CyberSitter, ContentProtect, and Cyber Patrol. The advantages of programs like these is that they are cheap (from $29.95 to $69.95), are able to be implemented immediately (as soon as you install the software, they are up and working), and have user-defined levels of protection (you may wish to have different settings, depending on whether you have a teenager or a preschooler). Another advantage is that they work with your existing ISP (Internet Service Provider), allowing you to keep your existing e-mail addresses.

Some of the disadvantages are that they may become outdated (and will require you to download and install updates), and can be disabled or circumvented by a determined child or teen.

Server-side filtering. These solutions filter the Internet (and other aspects of the online experience such as e-mail, IM, and news groups) before they enter your home. There are two different versions of server-side filtering: Filters that work with your existing ISP, and filtered (family friendly) Internet service providers. Let's look at each one:

Filters that work with your existing ISP. If you are happy with your existing ISP, you may want to consider one of the companies that offer add-on server-side filtering. Since you keep your current Internet service provider, you can keep all of your e-mail addresses as well. The filtering service usually costs around $5.00 a month, and may be cheaper if you pay by the year.

Filtered (family friendly) ISPs. Instead of keeping your commercial ISP (Internet service provider) such as AOL, Earthlink, or MSN, you may want to consider a "family-friendly ISP." These companies provide complete Internet access that automatically filters out objectionable Web sites. You will generally pay a monthly fee of between $13.00 and $24.00. Most offer dial-up (modem), but some offer high-speed broadband. Most will filter out all sexually oriented material, as well as other objectionable subjects such as gambling, hate groups, and so forth.

As with server-side filters, family friendly ISPs have some advantages over client-side software programs Here are some claims made by FamilySurf.net, a popular family friendly ISP, taken from their Web site:

Do I need special software?

No. Our filter is on our servers, so it blocks pages before they ever reach your computer. This allows us to frequently update the filter without the need for you to download updates on a daily basis. Just decide what you want blocked, and relax.

Why should I use your service when I can install filtering software on my computer?

First, our software is updated on a daily basis, insuring that you are as protected as possible. With your own software, you need to do daily updates to stay safe. Our software adds 300–400 sites a day to insure that you are as safe as possible. Managing that yourself would be a nightmare. Second, software filters that reside on your computer can be disabled, become out of date, or bypassed. In fact, there are a number of sites that tell kids exactly how to disable programs like NetNanny, CyberPatrol, and CyberSitter. Our software is on our servers and can't be disabled by anyone but the account owner. When you sign up, you set up a username and password for the filter. Only you can change or disable it.

What does S4F filter?

Family Surf's Filter, powered by S4F, blocks sites with pornographic or recreational nudity, sexually explicit language, or criminal activity. Criminal activity includes, but is not necessarily limited to, hate speech, wagering, illegal drug promotion, illegal weapons construction/modification/sales, and crime instructions.

It doesn't cost; it pays. You will pay slightly more for Internet access using a server-side filter because you will pay the monthly fee for your regular unfiltered ISP and an additional fee (usually monthly or yearly) for the filtering service. Yet, the extra amount you will pay is inconsequential in terms of the potential devastation that could be done to you and your family without such a filtering solution in place. It amazes me that many parents are content to sacrifice their children's innocence just to save a few dollars a month.

What do you get for the few extra dollars you spend? A lot. Here is a quote from Surf on the Safeside (www.surfonthesafeside.com), a server-side filtering provider: "When you subscribe to SurfontheSafeside.com, all your Internet browsing passes through our computers first. Each page is checked against a constantly updated list of blacklisted Internet sites. Using our technology, we are able to block over *240 Million inappropriate* or *illegal pages,* while allowing access to everything else. An immense amount of intensive labor is involved in the blocking process—100 people personally reviewing sites around the clock. *one million* new sites are checked every month."

One of the greatest advantages of server-side filtering is it cannot be turned off or tampered with.

One other caveat with family-friendly ISPs: The one you choose today may not be around tomorrow. Most are started by well-meaning Christian businessmen or organizations, but have a tendency to go out of business after a while. This is not meant as a criticism, but a simple statement of fact. Most family friendly ISPs are not money-makers and are operated more out of a "labor of love" than for financial profitability.

What should be blocked? Most filters, whether client-based or server-based, allow for some form of user definable levels of protection. A good filtering system will be intelligent in its blocking. For example, a filter set to block adult and sexual content typically will block sites that display nudity or depict sexual acts. It should not, however, indiscriminately prevent you from accessing legitimate Web sites on topics like sexual health, breast cancer, or sexually transmitted diseases. In addition to inappropriate sexual content, here are some other areas that a filter may target:

- Alternative lifestyles (gay, lesbian, bisexual, etc.)
- Audio and video file sharing
- News groups, chat rooms, and instant messaging
- Personals/dating
- Alcohol, tobacco, illegal drugs
- Weapons (guns, knives, bomb-making instructions, etc.)
- Gambling
- Hate groups

Although it goes without saying that you should block obvious pornography, you may or may not want to block some of these other areas as well. As you are making your choice on what type of filter to use, check to see if the filter you are interested in allows you to selectively block certain topics, or if it is an "all or nothing" approach.

Whose values? One danger to be aware of is that having someone other than you deciding what you should and shouldn't have access to is a form of censorship, which may or may not be a good thing, depending upon how close your personal views line up with the person doing the censoring.

For example, there is a real possibility that a Web site that takes a biblical stand against homosexuality could be labeled as a hate group site and blocked by some filters. If you choose a family-friendly ISP, choose one that has conservative, Bible-believing Christian values.

Parental controls. If you choose to use a software filter instead of a family-friendly ISP, there is another step you should take. Almost all of the major commercial ISPs (AOL, MSN, Earthlink, etc.) now have parental controls that you can enable. Most of the major Web browsers (Internet Explorer, Netscape, etc.) have parental controls as well. Most e-mail programs also now have spam filters that you can implement. Those work at varying rates of success.

You should take advantage of all of these, where available, but please take note: Parental controls by themselves are *not enough!* They must be used with some additional form of filtering software. As I said before, almost any parental control can be circumvented by a determined child or teen. Do not be lulled into a false sense of security by using them by themselves.

Will it work with my computer? Before you invest in any filtering solution, you should be aware that there is no such thing as a "one size fits all" filter. Due to financial constraints and technological issues, most filters work with only the most common computer set-ups. Most will not work with Macintosh computers. Some do not work with AOL. What are your best compatibility chances? A computer using a current version of Windows as the operating system, and using Microsoft Internet Explorer for Web browsing. If you decide to use a family-friendly filtered ISP, most, as of this writing, do not offer broadband speeds, only dial-up.

Many parents have avoided implementing filtering solutions because they potentially can slow down the speed of the Internet connection. Although I'm sure you, like everyone else, would like speed *and* safety, let me again implore you not to sacrifice your family's safety solely for the sake of a faster Internet connection.

Where do I start? As you can probably guess, you are not going to be able to walk into your local computer store and buy the filtering solution that fits your need from off the shelf. Where's the best place to find all the information you need about filters? The Internet, of course! To get started, you could type some of the following words into any search engine: *filtered Internet, family friendly, porn block, kid safe,* and such. The results will be hit-or-miss. Better results can be obtained by starting at the Filter Review Web site (www.filterreview.com) sponsored by my good friends at the National Coalition for the Protection of Children and Families (www.nationalcoalition.org). Many of the client-side filters have trial versions that you can download and try before you buy.

2. Block Unsolicited E-mail (Spam)

Unfortunately, even if you have successfully blocked all inappropriate sexual content on the Web, you still have to worry about e-mail. Many filtering solutions address e-mail as well as the Web, but with varying degrees of success. Although you are not likely to receive actual pornography via an unsolicited e-mail, chances are extremely high that you will at some point receive an e-mail from a spammer containing a link to a pornographic or inappropriate Web site. Spammers are also well known for sending out e-mails for sexual enhancement products and drugs. Needless to say, even if you never click on any of the links, you don't want to receive the e-mail in the first place.

So, what can you do to "can the spam"? Unfortunately, there is no easy one-click solution for eliminating unsolicited e-mail. If the Web filtering solution that you choose does a good job dealing with spam as well, great. If not, you may want to consider one of these three options:

1. Purchase spam filtering software (such as SpamWasher or Norton AntiSpam) for your computer (typing the words *spam filter* into any search engine will give you lots of options). Also, if you have not done this already, spend a few minutes to enable the spam-blocking controls that are provided by your ISP or your e-mail client. You may also want to subscribe to a spam-blocking service such as MailBlocks (www.mailblocks.com). This type of service uses challenge/response technology to insure that all incoming e-mail is sent by a human instead of a computer.

2. Use a family-friendly e-mail service like Kid Safe Mail (www.kidsafemail.com). This approach is similar to server-side Web filtering. According to the Kids Safe Mail Web site, "Every email your child receives goes through a six step cleaning process on our servers *before* it goes into your child's Inbox."

3. Use a "white-list" approach.[2] Using a service like Surf Buddies (www.surfbuddies.com), this approach allows your child to receive e-mail only from an approved list of friends known to your child and approved by you. (You can also do this yourself with most standard e-mail clients, such as Outlook Express, by choosing a setting or preference which only allows incoming e-mail from someone who is already in your address book.)

3. PRACTICE SAFE SURFING

There are two ways to encounter inappropriate sexual material online. Either it comes to you, or you go to it. If you take all of the precautions outlined in chapter 8—avoid news groups, chat rooms, and such, and install Web and spam filters—chances are rare that actual porn will come to you online. The much greater chance is that you will go to it.

How will you (or someone in your family) do that? By clicking on a link that you know you shouldn't click on, but you do anyway. That is why it is important to practice safe surfing. In fact, the practice of surfing the Web—clicking from one site to another, with no particular purpose in mind—is a recipe for trouble. You are much better off to get on, find what you are looking for, and get off. However, for those times when you (or someone in your family) are surfing the Web, here are some guidelines:

Make surfing a family affair. This doesn't mean that you have to be looking over your child's shoulder every minute, but experts suggest locating the computer in a central, communal area of the house. Ocean surfing is a great sport, but there is always the danger of undertow and sharks. It is sometimes dangerous to be out in the ocean alone.

Use a filtered search engine. When you search for a term in a search engine, you may find more than you were looking for. Even though Web filters prohibit you from going to the actual site, the description of a site might still come up in a search. Believe me, you don't even want to be reading the description. You have two options for filtered searching: (1) Enable the "safe search" controls on the commonly used search engines such as Google, Alta Vista, Lycos, and Yahoo. Most search engines have three settings: strict, moderate, and totally unfiltered. Although these built-in filters generally work well, none of them will give 100-percent safe search results. (2) There are also some filtered search engines designed for children. Here are some you may want to try:

- Dib Dab Doo (www.dibdabdoo.com)
- Stopdog (www.stopdog.com)
- SurfSafely (www.surfsafely.com)
- CyberSleuth Kids (www.cybersleuth-kids.com)
- Ask Jeeves For Kids (www.ajkids.com)
- Yahooligans (www.yahooligans.com)

When you start investigating family-friendly or filtered search engines, you will unfortunately discover two things: (1) The ones sponsored by Christian or family-friendly organizations are usually extremely limited in scope, and (2) the ones sponsored by the commercial Web portals are much more comprehensive, but do not support biblical Christian values.

For example, although Yahooligans filters out all obvious sexual references, you will find ads for Hollywood movies, rap and rock music, and information about astrology.

Be especially careful about so-called "kid friendly" search sites sponsored by libraries, public schools and universities, and government agencies. One such site, KidsClick (www.kidsclick.org), bills itself as "Web search for kids by librarians." A closer look reveals that its search engine is powered by technology developed at the University of California at Berkeley. Should that raise an eyebrow? Let's see.

A search using the term *gay* returns this site in the first position: "Be Yourself: Questions and Answers for Gay, Lesbian, Bisexual, and Transgender Youth." Here is the description of the site in the search engine itself: "Sexual orientation is one of the four components of sexuality and is distinguished by an enduring emotional, romantic, sexual or affectional attraction to individuals of a particular gender. The three other components of sexuality are biological sex, gender identity (the psychological sense of being male or female) and social sex role (adherence to cultural norms for feminine and masculine behavior)." By comparison, a similar search using the term *gay* in stopdog.com returns nothing.

Use directories instead of search engines. This advice comes from Internet Safety 101 on the Family Internet Web site: Another option is to use directories, such as About.com. Instead of searching, you go to the category you want information about. For instance, if you want information about Barbie dolls, you would go to the main page, select *hobbies*, then click on *collecting*, and then choose *doll collecting*. By using directories, you control what comes on your screen. Several search engines also offer directory options to locate what you are looking for. By contrast, typing the word *doll* into an unfiltered search engine would return some results you would not want to see.

Use online encyclopedias instead of search engines. Another way to find information on the Web without using a search engine is to use an online encyclopedia, such as Encarta (encarta. msn.com), Encyclopaedia Britannica (www.britannica.com), or Encyclopedia.com (www.encyclopedia.com).

4. PUT A FILTER ON THE TV

In addition to putting a filter on the computer, make sure you nail up the other snake hole—the television. Here are several practical solutions to consider:

I. You may want to consider installing a device called TV Guardian (www.tvguardian.com) on all of the TV sets in your home. It is a box that is hooked up between your TV and your antenna, cable jack, or satellite receiver. It uses the closed-caption feature that is in all broadcast TV shows and movies to read ahead of the dialogue. When it encounters profanity, cursing, or objectionable language, it either blanks it out, or substitutes a harmless euphemism on the screen. You can also install it between your VCR or DVD player and your TV. It works on virtually any video or DVD that you rent or buy. Some stores also sell VCRs and DVD players made by Sanyo and Fischer with TV Guardian technology built right in.

2. As I mentioned in chapter 6, if you have any premium movie packages that come with your cable or satellite service, cancel them.

3. If you have children in your home under nine years old, you may want to check out the Weemote remote control (www.weemote.com). It lets you program up to ten channels that you have preselected for your children to watch. Then you put away the regular remote control, and give them the Weemote. They can safely channel surf only the channels that you have preselected with their own personal remote control.

Protection Is Your Responsibility

By initiating these four safeguards—filtering the computer, blocking spam, beginning to practice safe surfing, and filtering objectionable content on TV—you will have taken a giant step in building guardrails to keep your family from falling. Remember, just as in Bible times, no guardrail will keep someone from intentionally climbing over it and jumping off the roof. However, the

Bible makes it clear that it is your responsibility, as much as possible, to keep your family from falling.

If this all seems overwhelming, do not get discouraged and "close down shop." Pray and persevere because the stakes are high and the reward is worth the effort. There is no cheap way or lazy way to do anything worthwhile. By God's grace you can do what you ought to do.

Endnotes

1. Andrea Petersen, *Wall Street Journal,* Nov. 6, 2000.
2. Unlike a blacklist, which blocks known spammers, a whitelist is more exclusionary in that it blocks all mail except that from the addresses on the list.

$\backsim$ **10** $\sim$

Involvement:
Time to Talk

T his chapter deals with the third step in our four-step battle plan—involvement. The previous two chapters— "Education" and "Protection"—contain powerful information that you need in order to begin the vital process of protecting your home in an X-rated world. This information must be studied carefully and applied prayerfully. However, in many ways, what is prescribed in this chapter will be much more difficult for you to implement. It will require courage and vulnerability, and at many times will make you uncomfortable.

Bottom line—it is time to talk. You may be a person who tends naturally to shy away from embarrassing subjects. You may have the type of personality that seeks to avoid confrontation at all costs. Nevertheless, your job as a parent demands that you talk openly and frankly with your family about the principles outlined in this book.

Cat Got Your Tongue?

Consider this story, entitled "Talk to Your Kids," as reported by *U.S. News and World Report*:

Most parents are silent, or close to it, on the subject of sex. Fifty-two percent of teens say their parents "rarely" or "never" speak to them about sex, according to a new Kaiser Foundation—U.S. News poll.

If you look for teachable moments, you won't have to look far. Sex is everywhere in popular culture. But stifle your impulse to interrupt a TV show to deliver a lecture. And don't just say, "That sitcom girl is a slut." Wait till the program is over, then ask your child what he or she thought of, say, the pregnant (and hastily wed) high school girl on the hit sitcom *Reba*. What would your child have done?

Parents *can* make a difference. In a study published in 2000, The National Teen Pregnancy Prevention Research Center analyzed interviews with 3,322 virginal eighth to 11th graders and their moms. Some teens had mothers who didn't disapprove of their having sex. Others knew their moms disapproved of them having sex at the time. At a follow-up interview after nine to 18 months, kids in the latter group were far more likely to be virgins.

Imagine that! Some teenagers still listen to their parents—even when the subject is sex.[1]

We Need to Talk

You may have never done anything like this before, but announce to your family, "We need to talk. We have some serious matters to discuss as a family." Then schedule some times to sit down with your spouse and kids and talk honestly and forthrightly about the issues addressed in this book. Notice I said "times." This will not be accomplished in one sitting. You need to plan a series of separate evenings where issues can be addressed individually. Make sure these are evenings when nothing else is planned, and there are no other events (ball games, favorite TV shows, meetings, etc.) vying for anyone's attention.

What will you talk about?

1. Discuss the problem of porn and the need for your family to protect itself.

2. Have a time where, as a family, you study the spiritual principles in this book, including "Learn to Think Like Moses," "Discerning Trash from Treasure," and "How to Have a Clean Thought Life."

3. Discuss the online trouble areas outlined in chapter 8, including the Web, e-mail, instant messaging, and chat rooms.

4. Discuss safe surfing, including the need to use appropriate searching techniques.

5. Talk about "stranger danger" online. If you still need some convincing about the potential dangers of online relationships, consider this story from *Light* magazine:

What if your child met a schoolteacher on the
Internet—would your child trust him? A teacher in
Culpeper, VA was recently arrested for possessing child
pornography obtained via the Internet. A former teacher
and coach in Birmingham, AL was caught in an Internet
child-pornography sting operation. Police found 100
images of children in various sexual acts on the home
computer of a high school band director in Jacksonville,
FL. Would your child trust a minister? An Arizona minister pleaded guilty to sending child pornography over
the Internet to a 14-year old boy. Would your child trust
a soldier? A former Fort Campbell soldier was convicted
of using the Internet to entice a minor to have sex.
Would your child trust a firefighter or police chief? A
Kansas City firefighter, 12-year veteran of the Orange
County, FL sheriff's office, and a former fire chief in
East Chicago have all been convicted of charges stem-
ming from Internet child pornography. Think your child
isn't vulnerable? Think again.[2]

6. Have an evening where you talk about the new family standards that you are putting into place. This would be a good time
to read and discuss Deuteronomy 22:8, the verse that talks about
building the parapet wall to keep someone from falling. Explain to
your kids that God holds you as a parent responsible for building
guardrails to protect your home. Go over the section on guardrails
from chapter 6 with your family, and talk about the guardrails you
are establishing concerning the following—the computer, television, Hollywood movies (both in the theater and ones you buy
or rent), and friends. Talk to your kids about the filtering system

you have decided to put in place on the family's computer (or computers, if there are more than one).

7. Talk about the consequences for violating the new "house rules" for computer and TV viewing. Agree that at the same time that each family member will be holding the other accountable, you will also be praying for and encouraging one another.

8. I suggest your final "talk time" be an evening where you talk about and sign the family covenant, as outlined in chapter 7. To celebrate the signing of the covenant, do something special afterwards, like taking the family out to eat to a place that your kids will get excited about.

Let Them Talk Back!

During the process, make sure your kids feel free to talk; they are on the team. To many parents, talking with their kids is a matter of "you sit still while I instill." Remember that good communication is a two-way street.

What will happen as you have these kinds of talks with your kids? You will:

- establish certainty,
- establish unity,
- establish accountability,
- establish vulnerability, and
- establish responsibility.

CERTAINTY

You will establish certainty as you set standards for your family. Vague opinion and half-hearted concern are not enough. God does business with those who mean business. Let your heart solidly believe and firmly trust. Be certain of the need and the promise of the Word of God. You as a parent must first establish your own convictions when it comes to what you will allow or not allow in your home. Then apply these standards lovingly, firmly, and consistently.

UNITY

You will also establish unity. It is so important to get the whole family on the same page. This may be your most difficult task. Be patient, be loving, be persistent. If your kids rebel, don't give up. Keep loving and praying. Don't make the war on porn the main focus. Love for Jesus and one another should be the main focus. There is no real spiritual unity apart from Jesus. Remember, rules without relationship lead to rebellion.

ACCOUNTABILITY

Accountability is a key factor in trust, and trust is a key factor in unity. When kids see their parents accountable to other members in the family, this brings a team spirit. This is part of a process: Certainty is built on the Word of God. This certainty brings unity. This unity is reinforced by accountability. Accountability puts all of the family on common ground.

VULNERABILITY

With accountability comes vulnerability. There can be no secrets in the battle against porn. Of course, there are limits to this vulnerability. You would not want to scar a child's mind by some confession in vivid detail. You might say, "I am having a problem in this area. I need prayer." However, when you become vulnerable to your family, they will do the same to you. It's hard to help when

You as a parent must first establish your own convictions when it comes to what you will alllow in your home. Then apply these standards lovingly, firmly, and consistently.

you do not know where the other person needs help.

RESPONSIBILITY

You must assume responsibility and teach it. But don't be a "lawgiver." Encourage your kids with words. Let them hear you say every day, "I love you" and "I am proud of you." Remember, the responsibility begins with the parents. If you do not have enough time for your children, you can be sure that you are not following God's will for your life. Here are some responsibilities that you ought to put into your life:

- Regular prayer attendance.
- Quiet time. Make it a prime time quiet time. Select the time best for you.
- Discipleship group with a gifted teacher.
- A personal ministry. You have enough Jesus to give plenty away.

You might assign corresponding responsibilities to your children, but remember to set the example.

Teach Your Children Well

To whom does God assign the primary duty of teaching his principles and precepts to your children? Not the church, not the school—but the parents. "And these words which I command you today shall be in your heart; you shall teach them diligently to your children, and shall talk of them when you sit in your house, when you walk by the way, when you lie down, and when you rise up" (Deut. 6:6–7).

At the same time as you teach your children rules of behavior, remember to teach them these vital truths about God:

- Hold on to God. Remember that he loves you. Nothing you will ever do is good enough to make God love you. He loves you by grace. There is nothing you can do to make God love you any less or any more. He loved you enough to send Jesus. That settles it.

- God does not love us because we are valuable; we are valuable because he loves us. He does not change us so he can love us, but he loves us so he can change us.

- He loves you just as you are, but he also loves you too much to let you stay that way.

In summary, get involved in the lives of your kids. Learn to talk. If your kids are uncommunicative by nature, do whatever you can do to tear down the barriers. Find out what they think is "cool," whether it is styles of dress or the kind of music they like. Even if you don't care for it, at least try to understand. When deciding what to allow and what not to allow, try not to confuse your own personal taste with something that is truly offensive, spiritually degrading, or immoral.

Take stock. If there are some changes that need to be made, make them. Above all, pray to God for wisdom. You will need it!

Endnotes

1. *U.S. News and World Report,* May 27, 2002.
2. Bill Parker, "Parents: Wake Up to the New Red Light District," *Light,* Fall 2000.

～ 11 ～

Awareness:
Knowing What's Going On

In the previous three chapters, we've covered: "Education: Are You Cyberliterate?" "Protection: Fences, Firewalls, and Filters," and "Involvement: Time to Talk." This chapter covers the final step in our four-step battle plan—awareness.

Awareness means that you as a parent must take an active role in knowing what is going on in the lives of your kids, including what they are watching on TV, what movies they go to, and what they view on the computer. It means you not only know what they are doing at home, but also at the homes of friends, as well as at school and the library.

This does not mean you are a spy. Your kids need supervision, not "snoopervision." It *does* mean you care enough to know where your kids are going, *and* where they have been.

Internet date cost girl her life, police say, the headline reads. Here are some excerpts from this chilling Associated Press story, dated May 22, 2002:

DANBURY, Conn.—13-year-old Christina Long was strangled by a married restaurant worker she met on the Internet. Her body was found early Monday in a remote ravine in Greenwich.

Saul Dos Reis, 25, an undocumented immigrant from Brazil, confessed Sunday to the killing and led law officers to the body, U.S. Atty John Danaher III said.

Police said the teenager routinely had sex with partners she met on the Internet and that she had been with Dos Reis several times, the *News-Times* of Danbury reported. Authorities found E-mail indicating that the two had agreed to meet Friday night.

Christina came to Danbury two years ago to live with her aunt, Shelly Rilling, after her parents divorced. Her father, Bruce Long of New Milford, said "there was no hint" his daughter was using the Internet to arrange encounters with men.

"I would give anything to take that computer back," Long said.

Your children's very lives may be at stake. It is more than a cliché to say, "An ounce of prevention is worth a pound of cure." Don't come to the time where you say, "Oh, if I had only done what I needed to do at the right time." Resolve to get started now.

I recommend a three-step approach: inspection, detection, and correction. These steps, if followed, will make a wonderful guideline for you. Remember that you are not the gestapo. You are a loving parent; but it is still your responsibility to inspect, detect, and correct. If you don't do that, who will?

Inspection

Many parents either don't care what their children watch and listen to, or they subscribe to the motto that "ignorance is bliss," evidently hoping to avoid confrontation and the conflict that may result. This is the same mentality that causes some "grown" adults to avoid going to the dentist because they are afraid he may find a cavity. The solution is to make an accurate assessment of the situation as soon as possible, so an intelligent decision may be made about any needed corrections. That is why inspections are necessary.

Before you begin, if you need to, deal with the notion that your children's bedrooms are "no-inspection" zones. Make sure your children have a clear understanding that anything they bring into the house is subject to the standards that you have set.

However, do not "search their room" without telling your kids first that you intend to do so. In one of the "talk times" I mentioned in the previous chapter, let your kids know that from now on, there may be inspections at any time of any areas of the house, including their bedrooms.

In fact, before the first inspection, I suggest giving them a head start. Let them know if they have something like a CD, movie, or magazine that won't meet the family standards of acceptability, they should "take it to the street" on their own.

Don't forget, you are not trying to "bust" them. How much better would it be for your thirteen-year-old to come to his own conclusion that "this rap CD I own has profanity, obscene language, and sexually explicit lyrics that dishonor God and my parents, and are unedifying for me to listen to. I think I better throw it away."

I do *not* advocate eavesdropping on your teenager's phone conversations or sifting through notebooks, purses, and desk drawers to read personal communication, such as notes and letters, even the romantic kind. As much as you may be interested, that is really none of your business. Make sure *they* know that *you* know the difference. You are inspecting the things that come into your home that may be questionable, unedifying, or immoral. You are not inspecting them. As I said before, you are not a spy.

What should you inspect? Here are my suggestions: the computer hard drive, all music, whether on CDs or stored in digital format such as MP3s, all magazines, comic books, and novels, all video or computer games, all movies, including VHS tapes and DVDs.

Where should you inspect?

- In your home—any areas where the above items could be found, including the bedrooms.
- Outside the home—homes of neighbors and friends (the things that apply in your home apply to the homes where your kids hang out, as well). In addition to homes of

neighbors and friends, I suggest you check out your local public library, the school library, and book stores (such as Barnes & Noble, Borders, and Waldenbooks), most of which have "age inappropriate" magazines and books on shelves within easy reach of children.

Right now, you may be thinking, "The library? Come on! What could possibly be wrong with the library?" Before you think I'm overreacting, I suggest you take a look for yourself. You may be shocked. Consider this warning by Karen Jo Gounaud, director of Family Friendly Libraries:

Danger Zone—The Public Library

In the beloved Meredith Wilson musical, "The Music Man," a beautiful but lonely librarian named Marian raised the eyebrows and voices of the local gossips because of some items in her inherited book collection which was now in the local library: "Chaucer, Rabelais . . . Balzac!" Those classics of academia are innocent as comic books compared to the realities of modern public libraries. What kind of songs would Wilson have to write today to include what is in contemporary library collections? What kind of Marian would proudly display raw pornography such as Madonna's *Sex,* Howard Stern's *Miss America,* or *The New Joy of Gay Sex?* The answer is, today's professional library leaders and trustees, carefully trained and directed by the American Library Association, will willingly place those tomes and other explicit adult materials in easy reach of your impressionable youth. Then there's the Internet, which libraries from coast to coast, also at the dictation of the

ALA, are opening to people of all ages. There are few if any safeguards between the users, even children, and Web sites of smut unimaginable to most well-meaning but cyber-clueless parents.

Those responsible adults who try to make or encourage common sense decisions are thoroughly berated by ALA leaders, liberal journalists and spineless politicians.

Families with borrowing cards at ALA-minded library systems can't even count on the librarians' cooperation in monitoring their own children's reading. The ALA discourages any policy that will tell an inquiring parent what is currently checked out on their minor child's card. But they are held responsible for the fines of damaged, lost or overdue books.

Even when a parent is constantly with a minor child, the children's book sections mix standard kiddie lit with sexually and violently explicit material for "young adults" that is peppered with profanity. An award-winning book is not necessarily a safe choice, either. The ALA controls most of the awards, too. Even kids' picture books often include copies of *Daddy's Roommate*, a gay rights pre-school publication. *Boys and Sex*, a sex education book "for 10 and up" by Wardell Pomeroy (a Kinsey partner), even has a written section encouraging kids to secretly consider sex with their pets as a normal activity.

In the meantime real classic literature and basic educational fare, such as books by Sir Isaac Newton, or even accurate history on the Magna Carta are getting hard to find. Except at library book sales. Balance is another casualty of the ALA-minded collection development. Most hot button issues of our times, like abortion, euthanasia, homosexuality, etc. are heavily weighted on the liberal and left sides of the debates. Conservative materials, especially Christian conservative materials, with an opposite perspective on those issues are much harder to find if they are there at all. Of all the new problems our wayward culture has brought into the American public library system, the provision of unfiltered Internet has been one of the worst. Even libraries that provide porn-blockers on the Internet units specifically reserved for kids usually also let the kids use the unfiltered adult machines. Easy access to illegal and harmful-to-minors cyberspace materials make unsupervised visits to the library especially unwise and dangerous. Open access has also proven to draw more patrons who are hard-core pornography users and occasionally even pedophiles. Yet ALA leadership, in unholy alliance with pornographers and the ACLU, make life very difficult for libraries and librarians that support the concept of blocking and filtering on library computer terminals. What can you do? Do not let your children go to the public library alone until you have verified that they have a functional filtering system on all of the computers that have Internet access.[1]

Detection

In the *inspection* step, you are informing yourself, possibly for the first time, of what is there that may be of concern. In the *detection* step, you determine whether there are any areas or items that are harmful, unedifying, or ungodly. This will mean that you will need to actually listen to some of the CDs your kids own, watch some of the movies they buy or rent, look through the magazine, and books, and play some of the video games.

In addition to things like magazines, movies, and music, you will need to make an assessment of what your kids have been viewing on the computer. In this section, I'll give some tips for detecting where your kids have been online.

When you surf the Internet your Web browser collects information about the places you visit and stores it on your computer. This information is easy to find if you know where to look. (It is also easy to delete, so be aware that many Web savvy kids do this on a regular basis.) There are three basic places your computer stores information when someone has been on the Internet: Web surfing history, cache files, and cookies.

WEB SURFING HISTORY

Browsers usually keep a history of sites recently visited. For Microsoft Internet Explorer (MSIE) users, there may be a button on your tool bar that says *History*. If this button is not displayed, then someone has probably configured MSIE to not allow browsing of the history files. If you see the history button, then simply click it to view recently visited sites. If you can't find it, go to *Help* and search in the *Index* for *History*.

Netscape users can search through the menu items across the top of the computer screen for a selection called *History*. If you're using a recent version of Netscape, you will find it in *Communicator* at the top of the screen. Click it, and then select *Tools*. Choose *History* and a list of Web sites, dates and times will appear. Or,

∽

Your job is not to catch your children doing something wrong, but to help them, to protect them, to pray for them, to love them.

∽

press the *Ctrl* (control) and *H* keys together on your keyboard to view the history.

Using either browser, you double click on the Web site name in the left column to visit any Web site listed in the history.

CACHE FILES

Browsers also make copies of the Web pages viewed and store them on your computer. This helps the browser load recently viewed pages much quicker than if it had to download the pages all over again every time you visited the Web site. These Web pages are stored on your computer and are called temporary Internet files or *cache files.*

Microsoft Internet Explorer (MSIE) users will need to find a menu item called *Internet Options.* Depending on the version of MSIE you are using, it may be found under the *View* or *Tools* main menu items. Once you have located this menu item and click on it, a box will be displayed with several "tabbed" pages. The tab page you want to use is the *General* page. Click on the button marked *Settings.* There, you will see another button marked *View Files.* Click on that button and you will see a list of all Web pages that are stored on your computer. You can double click on any file name in the left column to view it. If you use Netscape, simply type in *about:global* to get a list of recently cached files.

To find all Web pages stored on your computer, you can use a tool in Windows Explorer called *Find.* The easiest way to start the find function is to click anywhere on your desktop (screen) and press the F3 key. Or, you can find it listed in your start menu, if you click the *Start* button on your screen. Choose *Files or Folders.* When the find box is displayed, select the following options to search for Web pages stored on your computer. In the *Named* box type in: *.htm* *.html* (be sure to put a space between *.htm* and *.html)* In the *Look in* box select: *My Computer* from the drop down list. Make sure the *Include subfolders* item is checked.

The *Find* function will return a list of all Internet Web pages stored on your computer. Just double click on the file name in the left column (or icon if the results are displayed in icon format) and you will be able to view the file.

COOKIES

A *cookie* is a file sent to your Web browser by another Web site. Its purpose is to record your activities on that Web site when you visit it, so that next time you return, you can be presented with customized information. Cookies are regularly used by commercial Web sites and adult Web sites.

The cookie file resides on your computer, so you can look at it to see where your family has been. Use the *Find* tool (described above) to look for *cookies.txt.* When you find it, click on it. You will see a list of Web site URLs that have placed cookies on your computer.

BE A DAD, NOT A DETECTIVE

A word of warning: Don't get so caught up in "detection mode" that you start thinking like a detective and not a mom or dad. As I said previously, your job is not to catch your children doing something wrong, but to help them, to protect them, to pray for them, to love them.

But what do you do when you find something that shouldn't be there—an objectionable Web site, a dirty picture, an inappropriate online relationship? You apply the third step—correction.

Correction

We used to live in Merritt Island, Florida, which was next door to the Kennedy Space Center and Cape Canaveral. What a thrill it was to stand in our own backyard and watch those mighty missiles soar into space. Before a launch each of them had been programmed for a certain trajectory and pathway to follow. Few of them ever kept the original plan, but Mission Control would correct them while they were in flight and an inboard computer and gyro would nudge them back to the right track. This was a good missile, but it needed to be corrected.

Correction does not mean punishment, though sometimes that may be necessary. The best correction may be encouragement. We can correct by a word, by an admonishment, by a prayer time with our kids, and always by example.

God has constantly corrected his children. The victorious life is not a life of no mistakes. Rather, it is a life of fresh starts. God's mercies are new every morning. Remember that where there is failure there is always forgiveness and cleansing through the grace of God and the blood of Jesus.

The sooner the correction, the better. When you discover or suspect that anything is out of line, step in immediately. Indeed, if encouragement is not received, then a further step should be taken. Limitations can be put into place, privileges can be taken away, and restrictions may be laid down.

Dear parent, don't get discouraged and don't discourage your children. Correct them with wisdom and love. Be firm and be fair. One more time I want to remind you—these are your children. Don't sacrifice their moral life, their spiritual life, and perhaps their physical life on some idea that children are to be given total freedom and that you have no business in their personal lives. This is not true at all. You must do whatever is necessary to know what is going on in your children's lives.

Endnote

1. Karen Jo Gounaud, www.fflibraries.org.

～ 12 ～

Ready to Go MAD?

How You Can Make a Difference in Your Home

We've covered a lot of ground in this book, and now it's time to put it all into practice. I hope your heart has been passionately stirred to do something. In fact, I hope you're ready to "Go MAD"—Go Make a Difference. You must put this knowledge into action. "To him who knows to do good and does not do it, to him it is sin" (James 4:17). The sin of omission is greater than the sin of commission. Your knowledge makes you responsible.

Be a MAD Dad and a MAD Mom

In this battle, parents are a vital factor for good or evil. Sometimes a juvenile delinquent is a child acting like his parents. I can assure you that parents can make a difference.

Begin by getting your heart right. Make sure that you are not expecting any commitment from your family that you are not willing to make yourself. The consequences of pornography are just as devastating for a parent as for a child. You destroy fellowship with God, you destroy true love, and you destroy your family.

Once your heart is clean, start applying the action plan we have just been through in the previous four chapter—Education, Protection, Involvement, and Awareness. To help you follow through, here is a checklist of important steps. They do not all have to be done in this order, but check this list frequently to make sure you are not overlooking an important step.

1. Reread the chapter on Education—"Are You Cyberliterate?"

2. If you are not already competent in using a computer, set aside a day or evening with your spouse to become well acquainted with your computer, especially regarding going online. Do a quick inventory of online software that is installed on your computer, including Web browsers, e-mail programs, instant messaging programs, and news readers.

3. Reread the chapter on Protection, "Fences, Firewalls, and Filters," and purchase and install a filtering system for all the computers in your home. Put some type of spam filtering in place for e-mail.

4. If you have news reader software on your computer, trash it. If you have an e-mail program like Outlook, Outlook Express, or Netscape that is set up to subscribe to news feeds, disable them.

❦

The consequences of pornography are just as devastating for a parent as for a child. You destroy fellowship with God, you destroy true love, and you destroy your family.

❦

5. Cancel premium cable or satellite packages that have movie channels such as HBO, Showtime, and Cinemax. Block pay-per-view movies. Where possible, block objectionable cable channels like MTV. Consider buying TV Guardian (www.tvguardian.com), as mentioned in chapter 10, "Fences, Firewalls, and Filters."

6. With your family's participation, draft a set of "house rules" concerning the use of the computer. Here are some sample rules you may wish to include:

- Don't ever go to any Web site that has sexually oriented material or suggestive photos. Those that do will have their computer privileges restricted or revoked.
- If you find yourself on an inappropriate site by accident, or because you clicked on a link against your better judgment, close the browser window immediately. Tell someone as soon as possible. You will not be punished.
- Never download or install any files or software without permission (including IM or file-sharing programs).
- Never install or copy files or programs of any kind on the family computer that you have been given by a friend.
- Never fill out an online profile.
- Don't join any chat room or club without your parent's permission.
- Always keep the door open when you are on the computer.

- Never send a photo of yourself to anyone, or give out your real name, address, telephone number, school name or address, or your parents' names, work addresses, or telephone numbers.
- Never arrange for an in-person meeting with anyone you meet online.
- Never respond to any mean, harassing, sexually suggestive, or threatening communication.
- Don't download any music that doesn't belong to you. This is the same as stealing.
- Always feel free to tell your mom or dad about anything you read or see online that makes you uncomfortable.

7. Reread the section on guardrails in chapter 6. With your family's participation, draft a set of "house rules" concerning off-limits TV programs, CDs, musical artists, magazines, and such.

8. Establish a policy for movies that is the same in the theater, at home, and at friends' houses. An example: R-rated movies are always off-limits, PG and PG-13 movies may only be watched with previous parental permission. G-rated movies are generally okay to watch without first getting parental permission. Remember, you are accountable, as a parent, to know what is in the movies you are allowing your kids to watch. Don't forget that you can check any movie at a Web site like familystyle.com or gradingthemovies.com to find out why it has been given the rating that it has.

9. Have a "take the garbage out" day. Encourage your kids to come to their own conclusions that some CDs, videos, magazines, and posters that they own would not pass the "Jesus as a houseguest" test, and that they need to "take it to the street." If you as a

parent have questionable magazines and novels that need to go, lead by example.

10. Schedule and hold the series of family talks suggested in chapter 11, "Time to Talk."

11. Encourage every member of the family to begin memorizing the "100 Guard-Your-Heart Memory Verses" in appendix I (page 162). You may want to have a contest to see who can memorize the most. I suggest a substantial prize (like a bicycle) for each of your children who memorizes all one hundred verses. As I said in chapter 6, this is not a bribe; it is a reward. A bribe is an inducement to do evil. A reward is a recognition for doing good.

Sign the *family covenant* with all members of your family and exchange tokens of the covenant.

You Can Win This Battle!

As I have already told you, the devil has aimed all the artillery of hell at you and your family. He wants you to go down in flames. But you and your family don't have to end up as casualties on the information superhighway. I remind you that to succeed, you will need to help your family think like Moses—to learn to discern trash from treasure.

One more time I want you to consider the three great values: fellowship with God, the ability to love and be loved, and a godly and happy family. I bless you and your children with all of these. Let these be the great desire and goal for you and your family.

Remember that in setting goals for your children it takes more than a goal. It takes instruction and discipline. Success is achieving the right goals. Failure is to succeed in that which really does not matter.

Consider also that children really want more of *us* rather than the things that we give. Don't let your children have a dud for a daddy. Kids need and want structure in their lives. They want guidance from their dad. Obviously, too much structure can discourage. Don't make them say, "I can never please my father."

Indeed you can go MAD. You can make a difference—especially in your family. Remember that God is with you. He loves you and your family. He will enable you to guard your heart and protect your home.

Believe him for victory!

100 Guard-Your-Heart Memory Verses

1. Only take heed to yourself, and diligently keep yourself, lest you forget the things your eyes have seen, and lest they depart from your heart all the days of your life. And teach them to your children and your grandchildren (Deut. 4:9).

2. This Book of the Law shall not depart from your mouth, but you shall meditate in it day and night, that you may observe to do according to all that is written in it. For then you will make your way prosperous, and then you will have good success (Josh. 1:8).

3. Have I not commanded you? Be strong and of good courage; do not be afraid, nor be dismayed, for the LORD your God is with you wherever you go (Josh. 1:9).

4. And if it seems evil to you to serve the LORD, choose for yourselves this day whom you will serve, whether the gods which your fathers served that were on the other side of the River, or the gods of the Amorites, in whose land you dwell. But as for me and my house, we will serve the LORD (Josh. 24:15).

5. Be angry, and do not sin. Meditate within your heart on your bed, and be still. Selah (Ps. 4:4).

6. LORD, who may abide in Your tabernacle? Who may dwell in Your holy hill? He who walks uprightly, and works righteousness, and speaks the truth in his heart (Ps. 15:1–2).

7. The fear of the LORD is clean, enduring forever; the judgments of the LORD are true and righteous altogether. More to be desired are they than gold, yea, than much fine gold; sweeter also than honey and the honeycomb (Ps. 19:9–10).

8. He restores my soul; He leads me in the paths of righteousness for His name's sake (Ps. 23:3).

9. I will instruct you and teach you in the way you should go; I will guide you with My eye (Ps. 32:8).

10. Delight yourself also in the LORD, and He shall give you the desires of your heart. Commit your way to the LORD, trust also in Him, and He shall bring it to pass (Ps. 37:4–5).

11. The steps of a good man are ordered by the LORD, and He delights in his way (Ps. 37:23).

12. Oh, send out Your light and Your truth! Let them lead me; let them bring me to Your holy hill and to Your tabernacle (Ps. 43:3).

13. Create in me a clean heart, O God, and renew a steadfast spirit within me (Ps. 51:10).

14. Truly God is good to Israel, to such as are pure in heart (Ps. 73:1).

15. I will set nothing wicked before my eyes; I hate the work of those who fall away; it shall not cling to me (Ps. 101:3).

16. Bless the LORD, O my soul; and all that is within me, bless His holy name! Bless the LORD, O my soul, and forget not all His benefits: who forgives all your iniquities, who heals all your diseases, who redeems your life from destruction, who crowns you with lovingkindness and tender mercies, who satisfies your mouth with good things, so that your youth is renewed like the eagle's (Ps. 103:1–5).

17. From the rising of the sun to its going down the LORD's name is to be praised (Ps. 113:3).

18. I love the LORD, because He has heard my voice and my supplications. Because He has inclined His ear to me, therefore I will call upon Him as long as I live (Ps. 116:1–2).

19. How can a young man cleanse his way? By taking heed according to Your word (Ps. 119:9).

20. With my whole heart I have sought You; Oh, let me not wander from Your commandments! (Ps. 119:10).

21. Your word I have hidden in my heart, that I might not sin against You (Ps. 119:11).

22. Your testimonies also are my delight and my counselors (Ps. 119:24).

23. Incline my heart to Your testimonies, and not to covetousness (Ps. 119:36).

24. Your word is a lamp to my feet and a light to my path (Ps. 119:105).

25. Let everything that has breath praise the LORD (Ps. 150:6).

26. Trust in the LORD with all your heart, and lean not on your own understanding; in all your ways acknowledge Him, and He shall direct your paths (Prov. 3:5–6).

27. Do not be wise in your own eyes; fear the LORD and depart from evil. It will be health to your flesh, and strength to your bones (Prov. 3:7–8).

28. Keep your heart with all diligence, for out of it spring the issues of life (Prov. 4:23).

29. Can a man take fire to his bosom, and his clothes not be burned? (Prov. 6:27).

30. The thoughts of the wicked are an abomination to the LORD, but the words of the pure are pleasant (Prov. 15:26).

31. The words of a talebearer are like tasty trifles, and they go down into the inmost body (Prov. 18:8).

32. He who loves purity of heart and has grace on his lips, the king will be his friend (Prov. 22:11).

33. For as he thinks in his heart, so is he (Prov. 23:7).

34. As for you, my son Solomon, know the God of your father, and serve Him with a loyal heart and with a willing mind; for the LORD searches all hearts and understands all the intent of the thoughts. If you seek Him, He will be found by you; but if you forsake Him, He will cast you off forever (1 Chron. 28:9).

35. If My people who are called by My name will humble themselves, and pray and seek My face, and turn from their wicked

ways, then I will hear from heaven, and will forgive their sin and heal their land (2 Chron. 7:14).

36. Who can bring a clean thing out of an unclean? No one! (Job 14:4).

37. But He knows the way that I take; when He has tested me, I shall come forth as gold. My foot has held fast to His steps; I have kept His way and not turned aside. I have not departed from the commandment of His lips; I have treasured the words of His mouth more than my necessary food (Job 23:10–12).

38. You will keep him in perfect peace, whose mind is stayed on You, because he trusts in You (Isa. 26:3).

39. Your ears shall hear a word behind you, saying, "This is the way, walk in it," whenever you turn to the right hand or whenever you turn to the left (Isa. 30:21).

40. The grass withers, the flower fades, but the word of our God stands forever (Isa. 40:8).

41. Even the youths shall faint and be weary, and the young men shall utterly fall, but those who wait on the LORD shall renew their strength; they shall mount up with wings like eagles, they shall run and not be weary, they shall walk and not faint (Isa. 40:30–31).

42. For I know the thoughts that I think toward you, says the LORD, thoughts of peace and not of evil, to give you a future and a hope (Jer. 29:11).

43. He has shown you, O man, what is good; and what does the LORD require of you but to do justly, to love mercy, and to walk humbly with your God? (Mic. 6:8).

44. "Yet from the days of your fathers you have gone away from My ordinances and have not kept them. Return to Me, and I will return to you," says the LORD of hosts (Mal. 3:7).

45. Blessed are the pure in heart, for they shall see God (Matt. 5:8).

46. You are the salt of the earth; but if the salt loses its flavor, how shall it be seasoned? It is then good for nothing but to be thrown out and trampled underfoot by men (Matt. 5:13).

47. Let your light so shine before men, that they may see your good works and glorify your Father in heaven (Matt. 5:16).

48. You have heard that it was said to those of old, "You shall not commit adultery." But I say to you that whoever looks at a woman to lust for her has already committed adultery with her in his heart (Matt. 5:27–28).

49. Therefore you shall be perfect, just as your Father in heaven is perfect (Matt. 5:48).

50. The lamp of the body is the eye. If therefore your eye is good, your whole body will be full of light. But if your eye is bad, your whole body will be full of darkness. If therefore the light that is in you is darkness, how great is that darkness! (Matt. 6:22–23).

51. No one can serve two masters; for either he will hate the one and love the other, or else he will be loyal to the one and despise the other. You cannot serve God and mammon (Matt. 6:24).

52. But seek first the kingdom of God and His righteousness, and all these things shall be added to you (Matt. 6:33).

53. Enter by the narrow gate; for wide is the gate and broad is the way that leads to destruction, and there are many who go in by it (Matt. 7:13).

54. Not everyone who says to Me, "Lord, Lord," shall enter the kingdom of heaven, but he who does the will of My Father in heaven (Matt. 7:21).

55. But everyone who hears these sayings of Mine, and does not do them, will be like a foolish man who built his house on the sand (Matt. 7:26).

56. For with God nothing will be impossible (Luke 1:37).

57. "You shall love the LORD your God with all your heart, with all your soul, with all your strength, and with all your mind," and "your neighbor as yourself" (Luke 10:27).

58. For God so loved the world that He gave His only begotten Son, that whoever believes in Him should not perish but have everlasting life (John 3:16).

59. And this is the condemnation, that the light has come into the world, and men loved darkness rather than light, because their deeds were evil (John 3:19).

60. If you abide in My word, you are My disciples indeed. And you shall know the truth, and the truth shall make you free (John 8:31–32).

61. Do you not know that to whom you present yourselves slaves to obey, you are that one's slaves whom you obey, whether of sin leading to death, or of obedience leading to righteousness? (Rom. 6:16).

62. For those who live according to the flesh set their minds on the things of the flesh, but those who live according to the Spirit, the things of the Spirit. For to be carnally minded is death, but to be spiritually minded is life and peace. Because the carnal mind is enmity against God; for it is not subject to the law of God, nor indeed can be (Rom. 8:5–7).

63. And we know that all things work together for good to those who love God, to those who are the called according to His purpose (Rom. 8:28).

64. What then shall we say to these things? If God is for us, who can be against us? (Rom. 8:31).

65. I beseech you therefore, brethren, by the mercies of God, that you present your bodies a living sacrifice, holy, acceptable to God, which is your reasonable service (Rom. 12:1).

66. And do not be conformed to this world, but be transformed by the renewing of your mind, that you may prove what is that good and acceptable and perfect will of God (Rom. 12:2).

67. If it is possible, as much as depends on you, live peaceably with all men. Beloved, do not avenge yourselves, but rather give place to wrath; for it is written, "Vengeance is Mine, I will repay," says the Lord. Therefore "If your enemy is hungry, feed him; if he is thirsty, give him a drink; for in so doing you will heap coals of fire on his head." Do not be overcome by evil, but overcome evil with good (Rom. 12:18–21).

68. For "who has known the mind of the LORD that he may instruct Him?" But we have the mind of Christ (I Cor. 2:16).

69. Let no one deceive himself. If anyone among you seems to be wise in this age, let him become a fool that he may become wise (I Cor. 3:18).

70. Therefore let him who thinks he stands take heed lest he fall (I Cor. 10:12).

71. But thanks be to God, who gives us the victory through our Lord Jesus Christ. Therefore, my beloved brethren, be steadfast, immovable, always abounding in the work of the Lord, knowing that your labor is not in vain in the Lord (I Cor. 15:57–58).

72. Therefore, if anyone is in Christ, he is a new creation; old things have passed away; behold, all things have become new (2 Cor. 5:17).

73. I, therefore, the prisoner of the Lord, beseech you to walk worthy of the calling with which you were called (Eph. 4:1).

74. That you put off, concerning your former conduct, the old man which grows corrupt according to the deceitful lusts, and be renewed in the spirit of your mind, and that you put on the new man which was created according to God, in true righteousness and holiness (Eph. 4:22–24).

75. Therefore, putting away lying, "Let each one of you speak truth with his neighbor," for we are members of one another (Eph. 4:25).

76. Let no corrupt word proceed out of your mouth, but what is good for necessary edification, that it may impart grace to the hearers (Eph. 4:29).

77. And do not grieve the Holy Spirit of God, by whom you were sealed for the day of redemption (Eph. 4:30).

78. Let all bitterness, wrath, anger, clamor, and evil speaking be put away from you, with all malice. And be kind to one another, tenderhearted, forgiving one another, even as God in Christ forgave you (Eph. 4:31–32).

79. Finally, my brethren, be strong in the Lord and in the power of His might. Put on the whole armor of God, that you may be able to stand against the wiles of the devil (Eph. 6:10–11).

80. Finally, brethren, whatever things are true, whatever things are noble, whatever things are just, whatever things are pure, whatever things are lovely, whatever things are of good report, if there

is any virtue and if there is anything praiseworthy—meditate on these things (Phil. 4:8).

81. If then you were raised with Christ, seek those things which are above, where Christ is, sitting at the right hand of God. Set your mind on things above, not on things on the earth. For you died, and your life is hidden with Christ in God (Col. 3:1–3).

82. Therefore put to death your members which are on the earth: fornication, uncleanness, passion, evil desire, and covetousness, which is idolatry. Because of these things the wrath of God is coming upon the sons of disobedience (Col. 3:5–6).

83. But now you yourselves are to put off all these: anger, wrath, malice, blasphemy, filthy language out of your mouth. Do not lie to one another, since you have put off the old man with his deeds, and have put on the new man who is renewed in knowledge according to the image of Him who created him (Col. 3:8–10).

84. But above all these things put on love, which is the bond of perfection. And let the peace of God rule in your hearts, to which also you were called in one body; and be thankful (Col. 3:14–15).

85. Let the word of Christ dwell in you richly in all wisdom, teaching and admonishing one another in psalms and hymns and spiritual songs, singing with grace in your hearts to the Lord (Col. 3:16).

86. And whatever you do in word or deed, do all in the name of the Lord Jesus, giving thanks to God the Father through Him (Col. 3:17).

87. Abstain from every form of evil (1 Thess. 5:22).

88. But you, O man of God, flee these things and pursue righteousness, godliness, faith, love, patience, gentleness (1 Tim. 6:11).

89. Fight the good fight of faith, lay hold on eternal life, to which you were also called and have confessed the good confession in the presence of many witnesses (I Tim. 6:12).

90. For God has not given us a spirit of fear, but of power and of love and of a sound mind (2 Tim. 1:7).

91. Flee also youthful lusts; but pursue righteousness, faith, love, peace with those who call on the Lord out of a pure heart (2 Tim. 2:22).

92. All Scripture is given by inspiration of God, and is profitable for doctrine, for reproof, for correction, for instruction in righteousness, that the man of God may be complete, thoroughly equipped for every good work (2 Tim. 3:16–17).

93. To the pure all things are pure, but to those who are defiled and unbelieving nothing is pure; but even their mind and conscience are defiled. They profess to know God, but in works they deny Him, being abominable, disobedient, and disqualified for every good work (Titus 1:15–16).

94. For the grace of God that brings salvation has appeared to all men, teaching us that, denying ungodliness and worldly lusts, we should live soberly, righteously, and godly in the present age, looking for the blessed hope and glorious appearing of our great God and Savior Jesus Christ, who gave Himself for us, that He might redeem us from every lawless deed and purify for Himself His own special people, zealous for good works (Titus 2:11–14).

95. But be doers of the word, and not hearers only, deceiving yourselves (James 1:22).

96. Therefore gird up the loins of your mind, be sober, and rest your hope fully upon the grace that is to be brought to you at the revelation of Jesus Christ; as obedient children, not conforming

yourselves to the former lusts, as in your ignorance; but as He who called you is holy, you also be holy in all your conduct, because it is written, "Be holy, for I am holy" (1 Pet. 1:13–16).

97. Finally, all of you be of one mind, having compassion for one another; love as brothers, be tenderhearted, be courteous; not returning evil for evil or reviling for reviling, but on the contrary blessing, knowing that you were called to this, that you may inherit a blessing (1 Pet. 3:8–9).

98. Therefore, since Christ suffered for us in the flesh, arm yourselves also with the same mind, for he who has suffered in the flesh has ceased from sin, that he no longer should live the rest of his time in the flesh for the lusts of men, but for the will of God (1 Pet. 4:1–2).

99. By which have been given to us exceedingly great and precious promises, that through these you may be partakers of the divine nature, having escaped the corruption that is in the world through lust. But also for this very reason, giving all diligence, add to your faith virtue, to virtue knowledge, to knowledge self-control, to self-control perseverance, to perseverance godliness, to godliness brotherly kindness, and to brotherly kindness love. For if these things are yours and abound, you will be neither barren nor unfruitful in the knowledge of our Lord Jesus Christ (2 Pet. 1:4–8).

100. If we confess our sins, He is faithful and just to forgive us our sins and to cleanse us from all unrighteousness. If we say that we have not sinned, we make Him a liar, and His word is not in us (1 John 1:9–10).

∽ APPENDIX II ∽

Parent's Check List

Have you taught the principles in *Family Survival in an X-rated World* to your family? Yes __ No __ I Will __

"Be sober, be vigilant; because your adversary the devil walks about like a roaring lion, seeking whom he may devour" (I Pet. 5:8).

Have you made sure your heart is clean?

Yes __ No __ I Will __

"Blessed are the pure in heart, for they shall see God" (Matt. 5:8).

Are you praying for your kids?   Yes __   No __   I Will __

"Blessed is the man who fears the LORD, who delights greatly in His commandments. His descendants will be mighty on earth; the generation of the upright will be blessed" (Ps. 112:1–2).

Have you put up some guardrails?

Yes __   No __   I Will __

"Therefore, to him who knows to do good and does not do it, to him it is sin" (James 4:17).

Have you made and signed a family covenant?

Yes __   No __   I Will __

"Though one may be overpowered by another, two can withstand him. And a threefold cord is not quickly broken" (Eccl. 4:12).

Have you made the commitment to pay the price to protect your family, no matter what it takes? Yes __   No __   I Will __

"You therefore must endure hardship as a good soldier of Jesus Christ" (2 Tim. 2:3).

Have you made yourself accountable to family and friends?   Yes __   No __   I Will __

"Confess your trespasses to one another, and pray for one another" (James 5:16).

Have you taken steps to become cyber-literate?

Yes __ No __ I Will __

"Through wisdom a house is built, and by understanding it is established" (Prov. 24:3).

Have you cancelled offensive TV programming?

Yes __ No __ I Will __

"I will set nothing wicked before my eyes" (Ps. 101:3).

Have you exposed and let the air out of Satan's lies?

Yes __ No __ I Will __

"He was a murderer from the beginning, and does not stand in the truth, because there is no truth in him. When he speaks a lie, he speaks from his own resources, for he is a liar and the father of it" (John 8:44).

Are you trusting God for victory?

Yes __ No __ I Will __

"But thanks be to God, who gives us the victory through our Lord Jesus Christ" (1 Cor. 15:57).

A Suggested Internet "House Rules" Policy

Here is a sample set of Internet "house rules" that you may wish to adopt for your family. This list comes from Parry Aftab, children's Internet safety advocate, and author of the *Family Guide Book* (www.familyguidebook.com):

- People on the Internet can pretend to be anyone or anything they want. Don't let them fool you.
- Don't use bad language.

- Don't get into arguments with or answer anyone who uses bad language.
- Don't answer if someone says something that makes you feel uncomfortable or that you feel is "bad."
- If someone is doing something "bad," you should tell your parents right away. But don't turn off the computer or log out of the area where the person is doing something "bad." (The adult can then find the person and report his activities as a "terms of service" violation.)
- Use a fun name when you're online, not your real name (not even your real first name).
- Don't spend all your time online. Set limits on your computer use.
- Never give your real name, address, school, parents' names, friends' names, where your parents work, anyone else's e-mail address, or any telephone number to anyone.
- If anyone asks you for this information, don't answer him, and tell your parents or the adult in charge of the chat room.
- Never talk to anyone you met online over the phone, send them anything or accept anything from them or agree to meet with them unless your parents agree and are with you.
- Never show your picture online to someone without your parents' consent.
- Don't put any information in your online service profile without your parents' consent.
- There are places on the Internet where people talk about and show pictures of things we don't agree with. If you see

something like that, click the *Back* button and tell your parents.

- Don't do anything online that costs money unless your parents say it's okay.
- Never give out your password.
- Never give out credit card information.
- Don't copy other people's material and pretend that it's yours.